Northamptonshire Inspection and Advisory Service

Written by the NIAS Science Team

Geoff Allport	Judith Coley
Carole Creary	Des Dunne
Phil Garnham	Steve Harrison
Mick Revell	Gay Wilson

Edited by Des Dunne

Graphics by Jane Elliott

With special thanks to Jackie, Sadie and Jane for their endless patience in compiling this book

If you require training or consultancy about Sc1 contact the NIAS Science Team at Northamptonshire Science Centre 01604 750333

© NIAS 1996

ISBN 0 947590 27 7

GlaxoWellcome

Investigative and technical skills are the key to the success of science-based industry in the UK. As a science-based company, Glaxo Wellcome is therefore keen to support teachers in developing pupils' experimental and investigative abilities from an early age, recognising the importance of these skills to the Company's own long term success, and to the future science base of this country. Our support for The New Sc1 Book forms part of a continuing programme of charitable contributions which places special emphasis on scientific and medical education, as well as healthcare. We hope the book will prove to be a valuable resource in supporting an important part of the science curriculum.

Where to Find Things in this Book

Understanding the nature of the scientific process
pages 2 - 24

How to initiate experiments and investigations with children
pages 54 - 64

Handling factors or variables
pages 39 - 46

Helping children to assess their own progress
pages 106 - 112

I think the blue ball is the better bouncer

Increasing the height gives the ball more energy; but are these measurements reliable enough?

Age 5 ⟶ Age 16

Increasing level of experimental and investigative complexity and demand

Using assessment formatively
pages 83 - 104

Helping children to progress
pages 72 - 90

Classroom management of practical activities
pages 54 - 64

Recognising levels of attainment
pages 92 - 104

Progression in Sc1
pages 26 - 38

Contents

page		
1	**Chapter 1**	**What is Experimental and Investigative Science?** understanding the nature of the scientific process
15	**Chapter 2**	**Experimental and Investigative Science Exemplified** examples of the experimental and investigative science continuum explained in text and diagrams
25	**Chapter 3**	**Progression In Experimental and Investigative Science** an analysis of progression within experimental and investigative science
39	**Chapter 4**	**What Are Factors or Variables?** an explanation of factors and variables including their role in experimental and investigative science
47	**Chapter 5**	**Planning Experimental and Investigative Learning** the principles of planning for effective practical work
53	**Chapter 6**	**Managing Experimental and Investigative Learning** distinguishing features of managing experimental practical work and managing investigative learning
65	**Chapter 7**	**Organising Classrooms and Resources** how to organise equipment and classrooms including planning for safety
71	**Chapter 8**	**Strategies for Teacher Intervention During Experimental and Investigative Science Activities** using teachers' skills to improve children's learning
91	**Chapter 9**	**How Can We Recognise Attainment in Sc1?** assessing achievement at all levels of Sc1
105	**Chapter 10**	**How Can We Help Children To Assess Their Own Progress?** helping children help themselves in Sc1

Chapter 1

What Is Experimental and Investigative Science?

page   2   What is Experimental and Investigative Science?
             4   A Simple Investigation
             6   How this Simple Investigation Meets the Requirements of the National Curriculum
             7   The Scientific Process
             8   The Most Significant Changes to Sc1 in the 1995 Curriculum for England and Wales
             9   Implications of the New Sc1 for Teachers and Learning in Science Lessons
           10   Explanation of Some Terms
           11   How the Scientific Process Fits the Programme of Study for Sc1

What is Experimental and Investigative Science?

Changes in attainment target 1 (Sc1) have resulted in a shift of emphasis between developing and assessing discrete skills and developing and assessing whole investigations. The 1995 Science Orders for England and Wales strike a new balance between experimental and investigative work which is reflected in the new name of the attainment target.

Managing Sc1

Previous models of Sc1 have presented considerable challenges to teachers, even those with strong subject knowledge, in managing and assessing children's learning. Enabling children to do independent investigative work requires subtle and supportive classroom management where children are guided and their thinking refined through questioning. By contrast, the direct teaching of discrete skills and training children in investigative procedures using illustrative (practical) work are more teacher led.

Sc1 is now designed:

- to enable children to master scientific methodology and undertake their own investigations

- to provide a context for the acquisition of knowledge or understanding

- to develop particular technical skills such as using a microscope, hand lens or measuring equipment

These may be initiated by the teacher or undertaken by the children as experiments or investigations.

Children's Independence

All practical science can be considered as a continuum with heavily directed illustrative work and totally independent investigative work at its extremes.

heavily directed illustrative work (experimental) ⟵⟶ totally independent investigative work

experiments using practical skills — individual or group investigation

Assessment Issues

Children's achievements in Sc1 can be assessed in a wide range of contexts. We believe that learning and assessment best take place within contexts that are deliberately and clearly related to whole investigations. While it is technically possible to assess pupils using specific aspects such as:

- planning
- observing
- measuring
- analysing results

we regard this as limiting the key entitlement which Sc1 gives children, ie to become scientific thinkers who can apply:

- mathematical
- linguistic
- observational
- logical

skills to investigating scientific ideas or events.

It is important that the complete scientific process is recognised as the foundation upon which the assessment of experimental and investigative science takes place.

This book is about:

- helping teachers to develop all aspects of science in teaching investigative and practical work
- providing support to all who teach investigative and practical science

The book details the management of children's learning through the different stages of the scientific process whether it takes place in experiments, investigations or aspects of investigations.

This is illustrated by the simple practical investigation of bubbles on the following three pages.

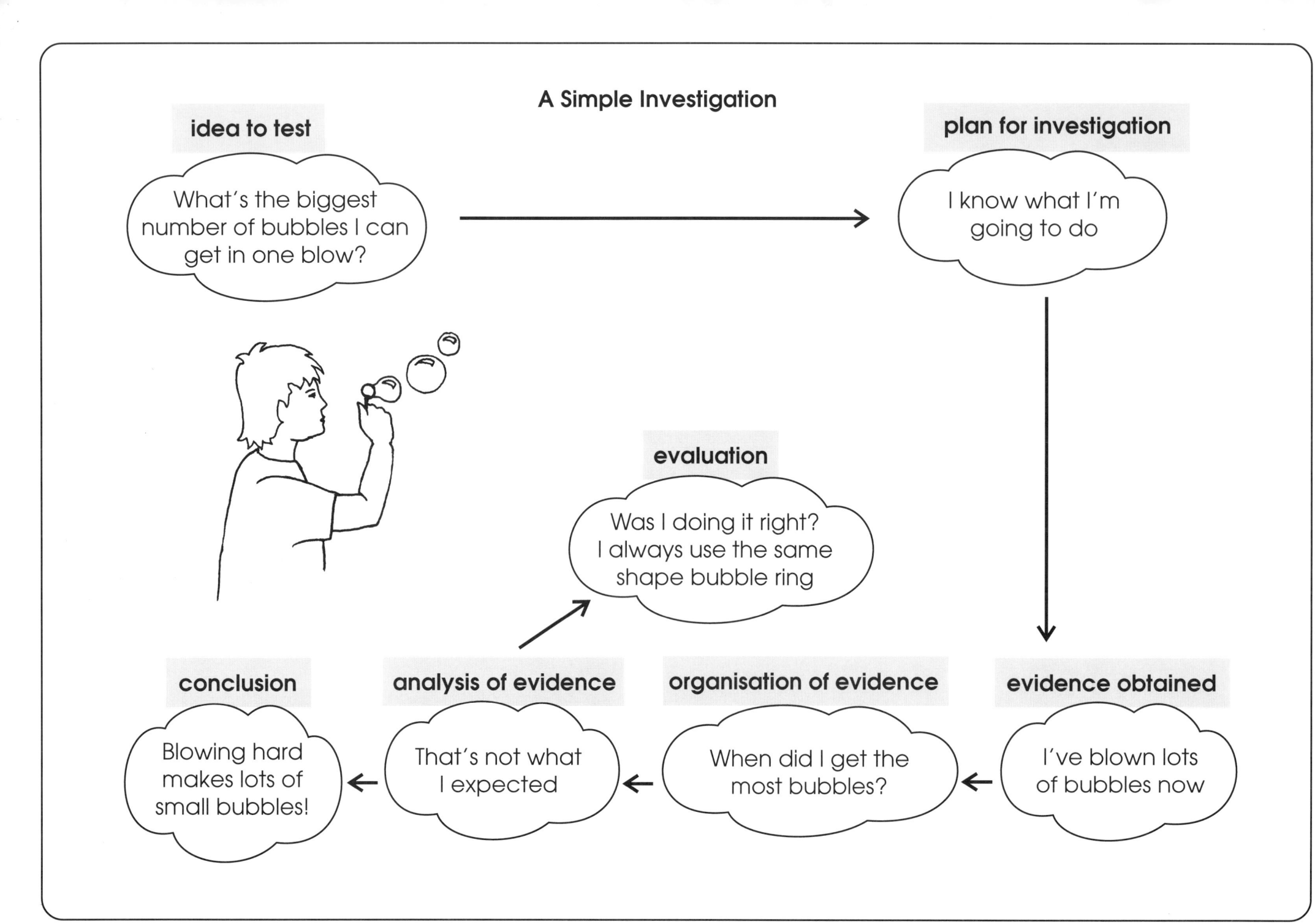

A Simple Investigation

idea to test
What's the biggest number of bubbles I can get in one blow?

→

plan for investigation
I know what I'm going to do

↓

evidence obtained
I've blown lots of bubbles now

←

organisation of evidence
When did I get the most bubbles?

←

analysis of evidence
That's not what I expected

←

conclusion
Blowing hard makes lots of small bubbles!

evaluation
Was I doing it right? I always use the same shape bubble ring

That Same Investigation Set Out Schematically

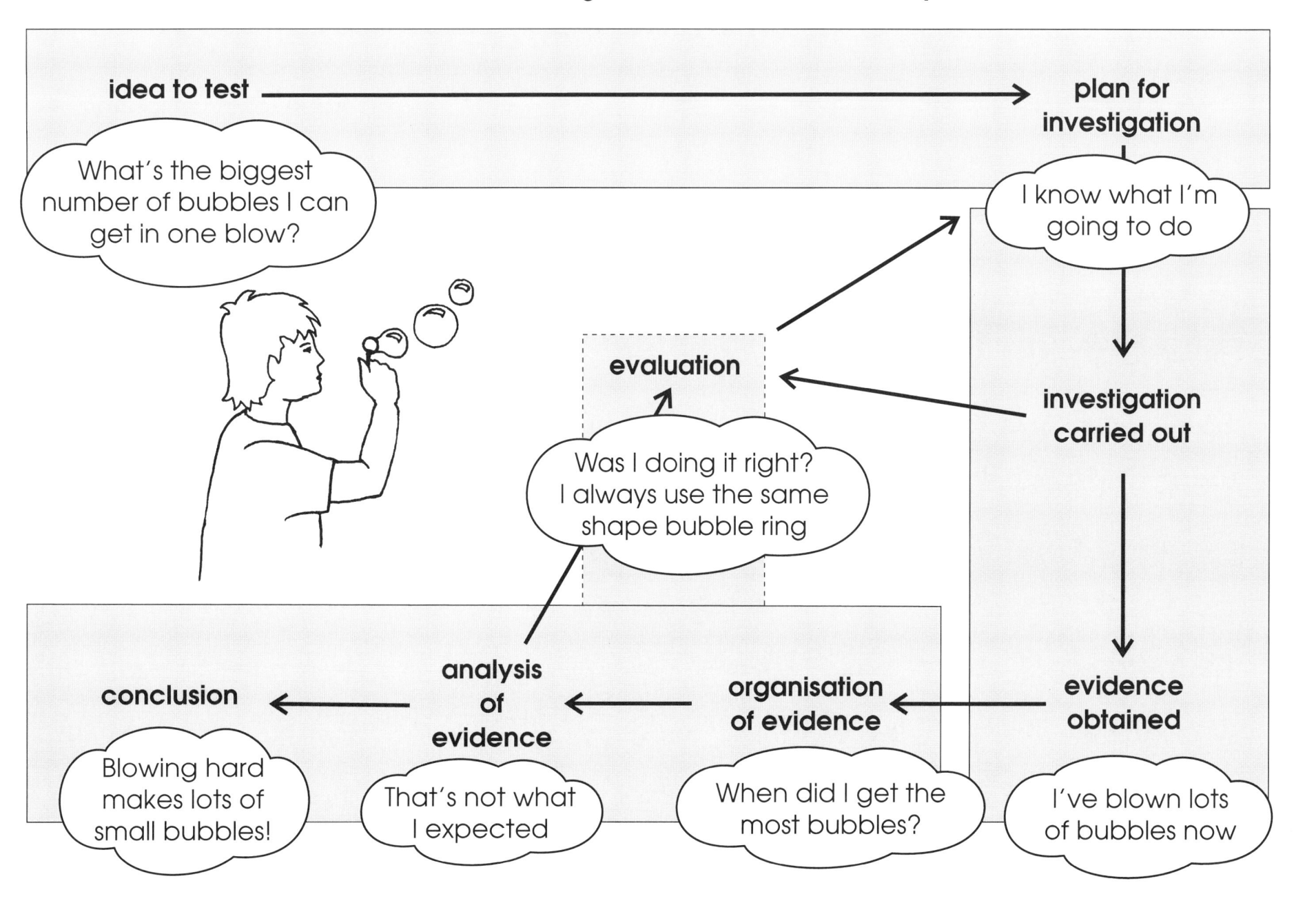

idea to test → **plan for investigation**

What's the biggest number of bubbles I can get in one blow?

I know what I'm going to do

↓

investigation carried out

↓

evidence obtained — *I've blown lots of bubbles now*

←

organisation of evidence — *When did I get the most bubbles?*

←

analysis of evidence — *That's not what I expected*

←

conclusion — *Blowing hard makes lots of small bubbles!*

evaluation — *Was I doing it right? I always use the same shape bubble ring*

How this Simple Investigation Meets the Requirements of the National Curriculum

PLANNING EXPERIMENTAL PROCEDURES (Sc1 - 1a, b, c...)

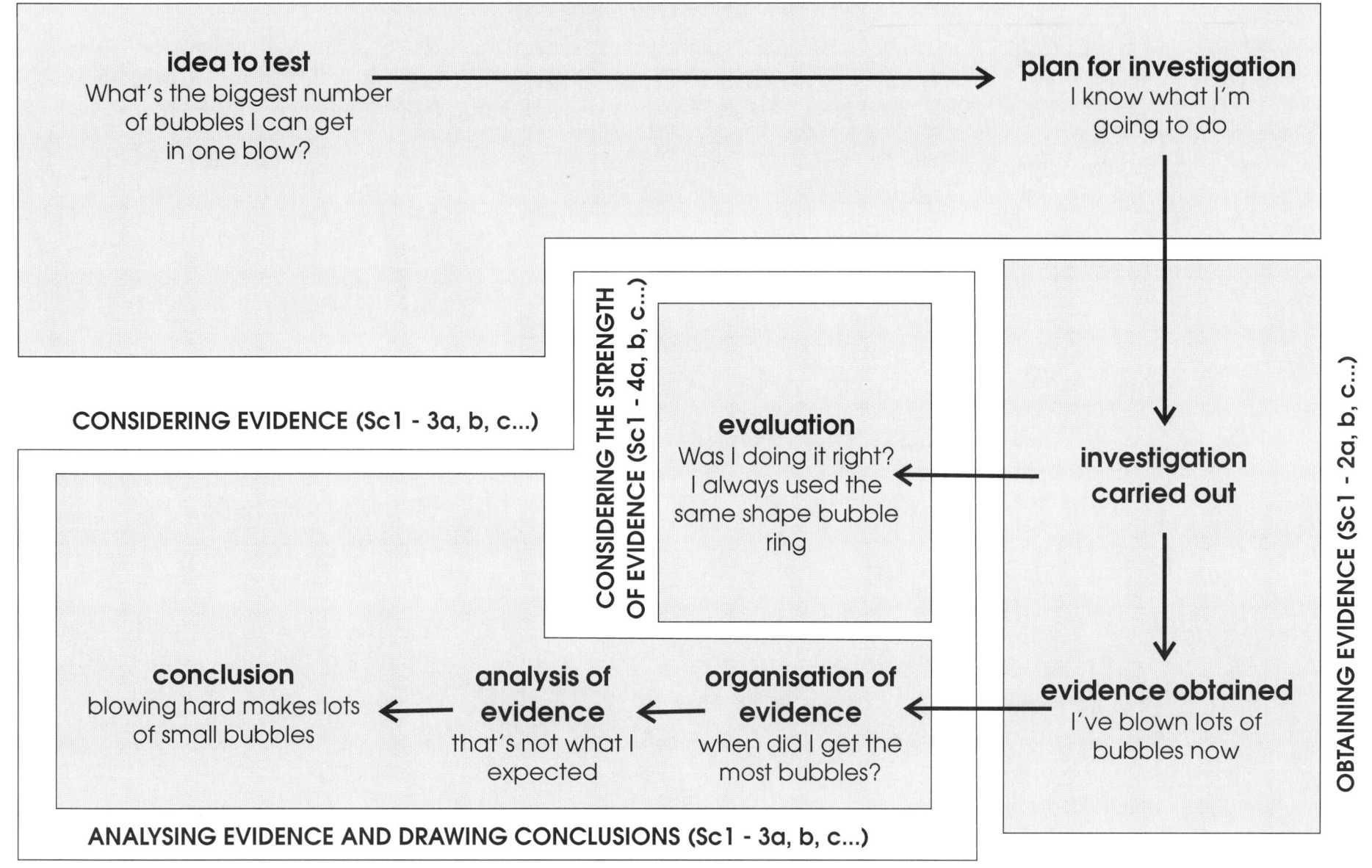

idea to test
What's the biggest number of bubbles I can get in one blow?

→ **plan for investigation**
I know what I'm going to do

CONSIDERING EVIDENCE (Sc1 - 3a, b, c...)

CONSIDERING THE STRENGTH OF EVIDENCE (Sc1 - 4a, b, c...)

evaluation
Was I doing it right? I always used the same shape bubble ring

OBTAINING EVIDENCE (Sc1 - 2a, b, c...)

investigation carried out

evidence obtained
I've blown lots of bubbles now

conclusion
blowing hard makes lots of small bubbles

← **analysis of evidence**
that's not what I expected

← **organisation of evidence**
when did I get the most bubbles?

ANALYSING EVIDENCE AND DRAWING CONCLUSIONS (Sc1 - 3a, b, c...)

The secondary science National Curriculum consists of four sub-headings (the four shaded boxes)
The primary science National Curriculum consists of three sub-headings (the third sub-heading accounts for two shaded boxes in the bottom left hand corner)

The Scientific Process

PLANNING EXPERIMENTAL PROCEDURES

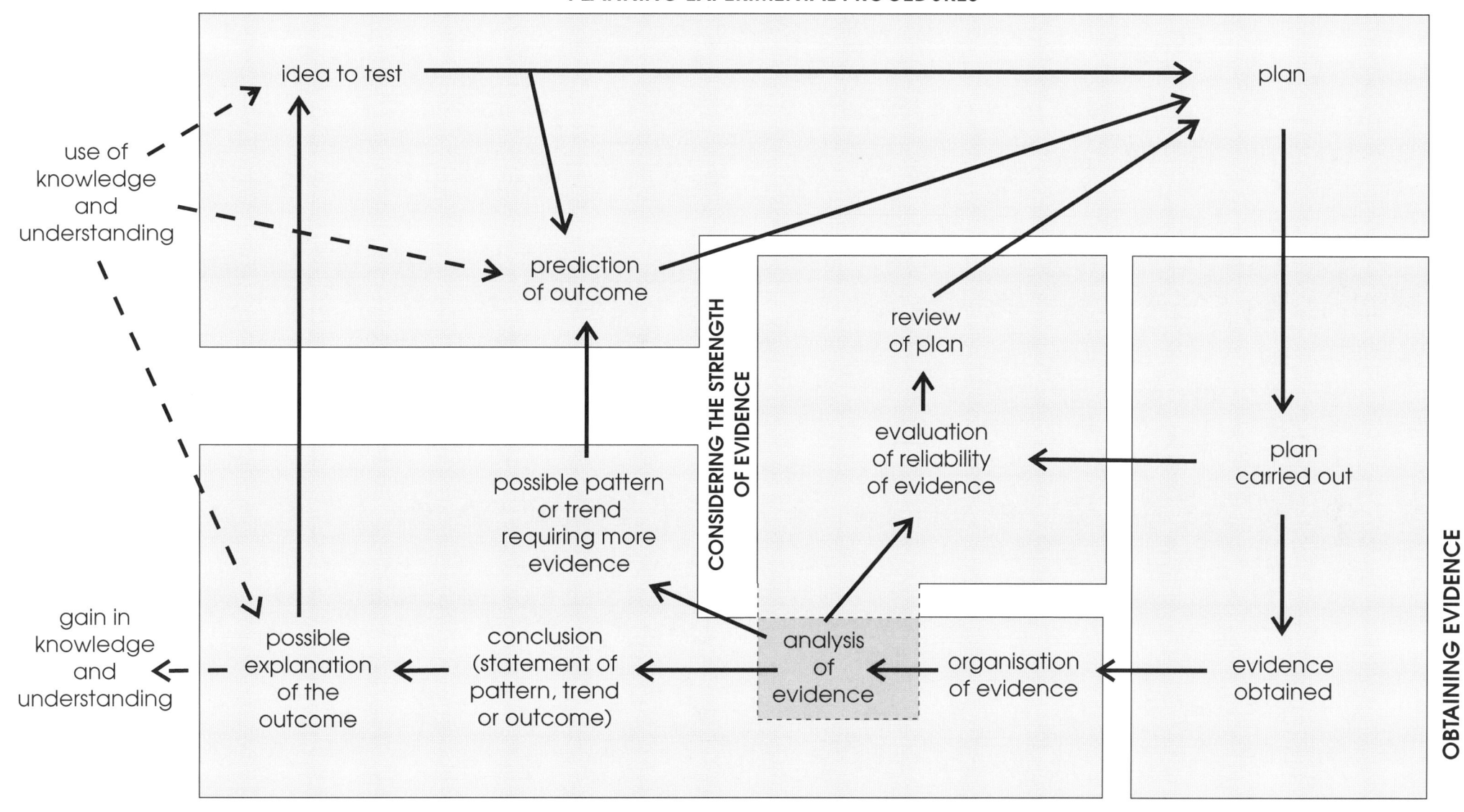

- idea to test
- plan
- use of knowledge and understanding
- prediction of outcome
- review of plan
- evaluation of reliability of evidence
- plan carried out
- possible pattern or trend requiring more evidence
- gain in knowledge and understanding
- possible explanation of the outcome
- conclusion (statement of pattern, trend or outcome)
- analysis of evidence
- organisation of evidence
- evidence obtained

CONSIDERING THE STRENGTH OF EVIDENCE

OBTAINING EVIDENCE

ANALYSING EVIDENCE AND DRAWING CONCLUSIONS

The Most Significant Changes to Sc1 in the 1995 Curriculum for England and Wales

Investigative Science 1992 - 1995	Experimental and Investigative Science 1995
• expectation that children complete all aspects of an investigation	• facility for developing aspects of experimental and investigational ability within the scientific process cycle
• expectation that only whole investigations are assessed	• range of activities from teacher directed experiments to investigations by children can be assessed
• summative assessment is usually based on performance in a few discrete investigations	• summative assessment is based on overall performance across a wide range of contexts
• teacher required to manage only whole investigation work	• teacher can decide to focus on one aspect of scientific process cycle
• expectation that children undertake whole investigations at all ages and levels of ability	• all aspects of the scientific process are not always required
• usually starts with an idea to test or hypothesis	• can start the practical activity at several places in the scientific process cycle
• requirements to make a prediction	• prediction is optional, not a requirement
• emphasis on identifying and controlling variables	• consideration of factors is less restricting than control of variables
• emphasis on quantification at higher levels	• the need for quantification is less explicit
• evaluation and conclusion assumed to be the same activity	• more explicit role for evaluation of reliabilty of evidence and conclusions drawn from that evidence
• expectation that scientific knowledge and understanding must be known at start by older pupils	• both the gain in scientific knowledge and understanding and its use are recognised

Implications of the New Sc1 for Teachers and Learning in Science Lessons

Teachers of science will need to:

- review all practical activities in schemes of work to identify purpose and learning objectives

- decide which practical activities are to be used for the assessment of Sc1 indicating those that will focus on aspects of the scientific process and those that will focus on the whole process

- plan the progressive increase in range and scope of practical activities within and across the key stages

- identify the management issues of each type of selected practical activity, ie will the whole scientific process be needed or will it be appropriate to select only part of the process?

- emphasise the place that a restricted practical exercise has within the whole cycle of the scientific process even when taught as a single practical activity

- plan the progressive development of skills and processes within and across the key stages

- decide whether asking for a prediction is appropriate during any practical activity

- be aware that biological practical activities and fieldwork can now be more easily assessed as part of Sc1

- decide whether quantification is appropriate during each piece of practical activity

- plan strategies and opportunities in practical activities for the development of skills in evaluating evidence collected and the reliability of conclusions drawn from the evidence

- decide whether it is appropriate to base a piece of practical activity on prior scientific knowledge and understanding

Explanation of Some Terms and How the Scientific Process Relates to the National Curriculum

Experimental and Investigative Science provides pupils with a programme designed to help them develop a scientific approach to their learning. In the simplest terms, it enables pupils to **propose explanations** and to **find things out**. Proposing explanations includes the predicting aspect of **planning and analysing evidence and drawing conclusions**. Finding out includes most of **planning, obtaining evidence** and **considering the strength of evidence**. Effectively, the left hand side of this page is about proposing explanations, while the right hand side is concerned with the skills of finding out.

Proposing Explanations

Hypothesising, inferring and predicting can all be viewed as one type of intellectual activity, that of proposing explanations, and are delineated by the different degree of certainty of the proposed explanation.

Hypotheses look forward:
a hypothesis is an informed guess and can be refined into an idea that can be tested.

Inferences (conclusion) look backwards:
an inference is a suggested explanation based on evidence (which can lead to further testable hypotheses). Most investigations should lead to a variety of inferences. The term "inference" is preferable to "conclusion" as it does not imply such a high degree of certainty, nor does it have that false air of finality.

Predictions look backwards then forwards:
predictions are based on much evidence, where a pattern is gained from repeated experiments. Predictions are only made when there is a higher degree of certainty.
Predictions, like hypotheses, are testable.
(Within the Programmes of Study the word "prediction" is used more loosely, with a much smaller base of experimental evidence and a larger component of guess-work.)

Finding Out

(Skills employed by and developed through the scientific process)

Observation (obtaining evidence) from noting basic sensory information to refined observation using equipment. Observation will lead to classification.

Measurement (obtaining evidence) from non-standard to standard units with increasing accuracy.

Identifying and manipulating variables (planning experimental work) from simple identification of factors and categoric variables to larger numbers of increasingly complex varieties of variables.

Communicating (preamble to each key stage) from simple talking to multi-media approaches.

Researching (preamble to each key stage) from looking at objects, to using libraries, to interrogating electronic data bases.

Interpreting (considering, analysing and evaluating evidence) from noticing that blowing hard makes lots of small bubbles to more complex questions of validity and reliability of evidence.

How the scientific process relates to each key stage Programme of Study is provided on the next four pages

How the Scientific Process Fits the Programme of Study for Sc1

Key Stage One

Statements from the National Curriculum are in bold
The scientific process is illustrated in the background in shade

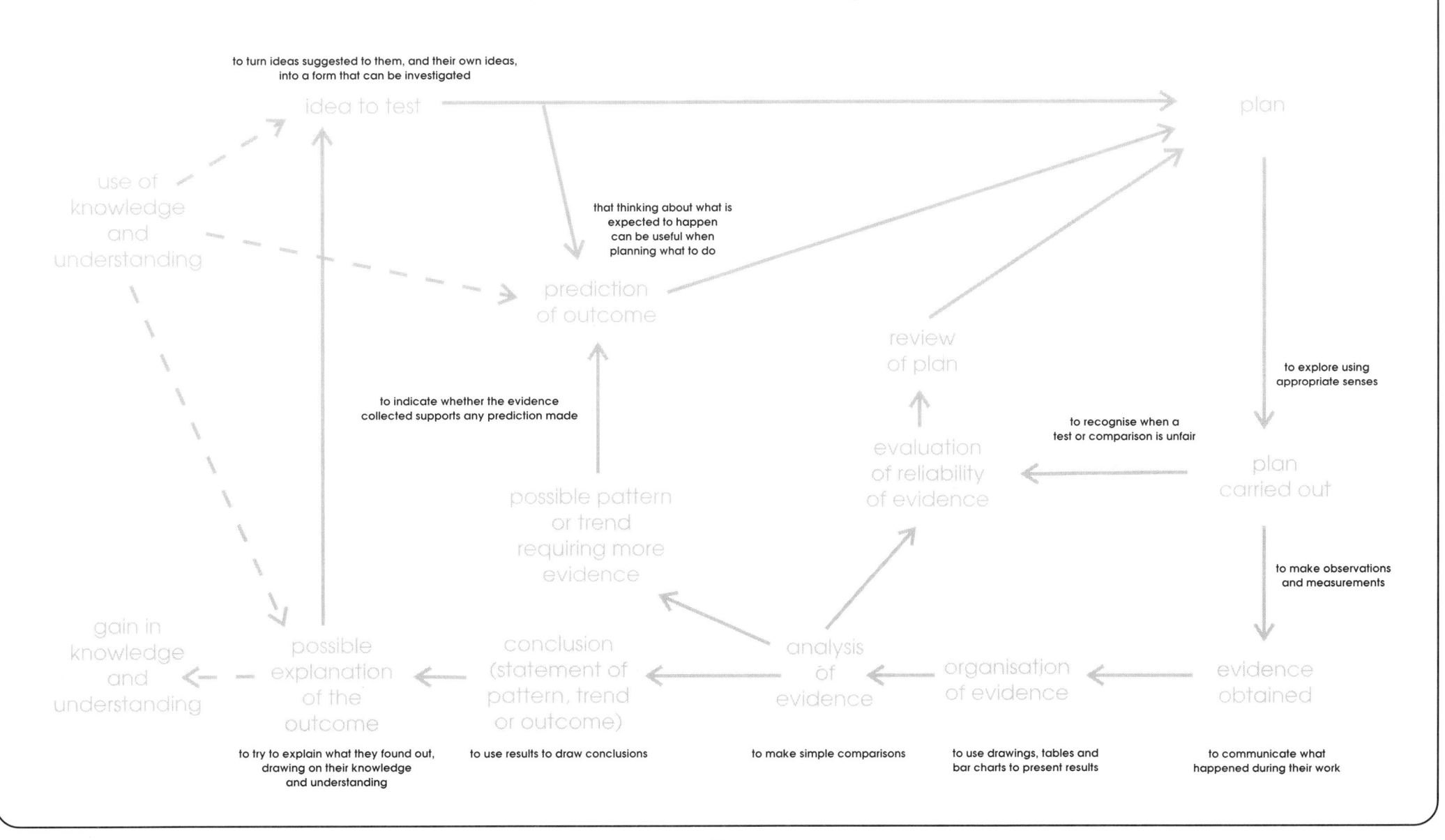

to turn ideas suggested to them, and their own ideas, into a form that can be investigated

idea to test → plan

use of knowledge and understanding

that thinking about what is expected to happen can be useful when planning what to do

prediction of outcome

review of plan

to explore using appropriate senses

to indicate whether the evidence collected supports any prediction made

evaluation of reliability of evidence

to recognise when a test or comparison is unfair

plan carried out

possible pattern or trend requiring more evidence

to make observations and measurements

gain in knowledge and understanding ← possible explanation of the outcome ← conclusion (statement of pattern, trend or outcome) ← analysis of evidence ← organisation of evidence ← evidence obtained

to try to explain what they found out, drawing on their knowledge and understanding

to use results to draw conclusions

to make simple comparisons

to use drawings, tables and bar charts to present results

to communicate what happened during their work

How the Scientific Process Fits the Programme of Study for Sc1
Key Stage Two

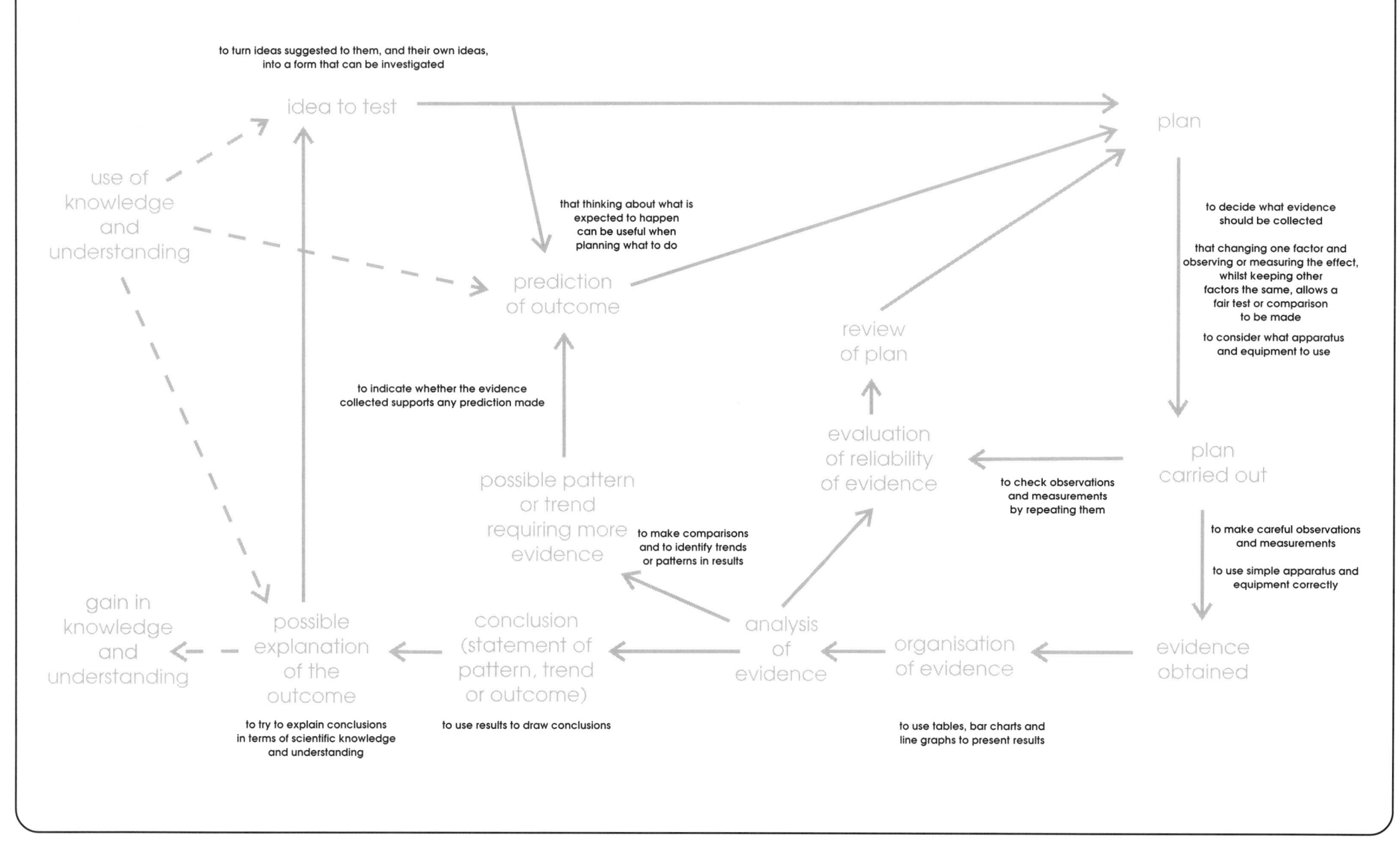

use of knowledge and understanding

to turn ideas suggested to them, and their own ideas, into a form that can be investigated

idea to test

plan

that thinking about what is expected to happen can be useful when planning what to do

to decide what evidence should be collected

that changing one factor and observing or measuring the effect, whilst keeping other factors the same, allows a fair test or comparison to be made

to consider what apparatus and equipment to use

prediction of outcome

review of plan

to indicate whether the evidence collected supports any prediction made

evaluation of reliability of evidence

plan carried out

to check observations and measurements by repeating them

possible pattern or trend requiring more evidence

to make comparisons and to identify trends or patterns in results

to make careful observations and measurements

to use simple apparatus and equipment correctly

gain in knowledge and understanding

possible explanation of the outcome

conclusion (statement of pattern, trend or outcome)

analysis of evidence

organisation of evidence

evidence obtained

to try to explain conclusions in terms of scientific knowledge and understanding

to use results to draw conclusions

to use tables, bar charts and line graphs to present results

How the Scientific Process Fits the Programme of Study for Sc1
Key Stage Three

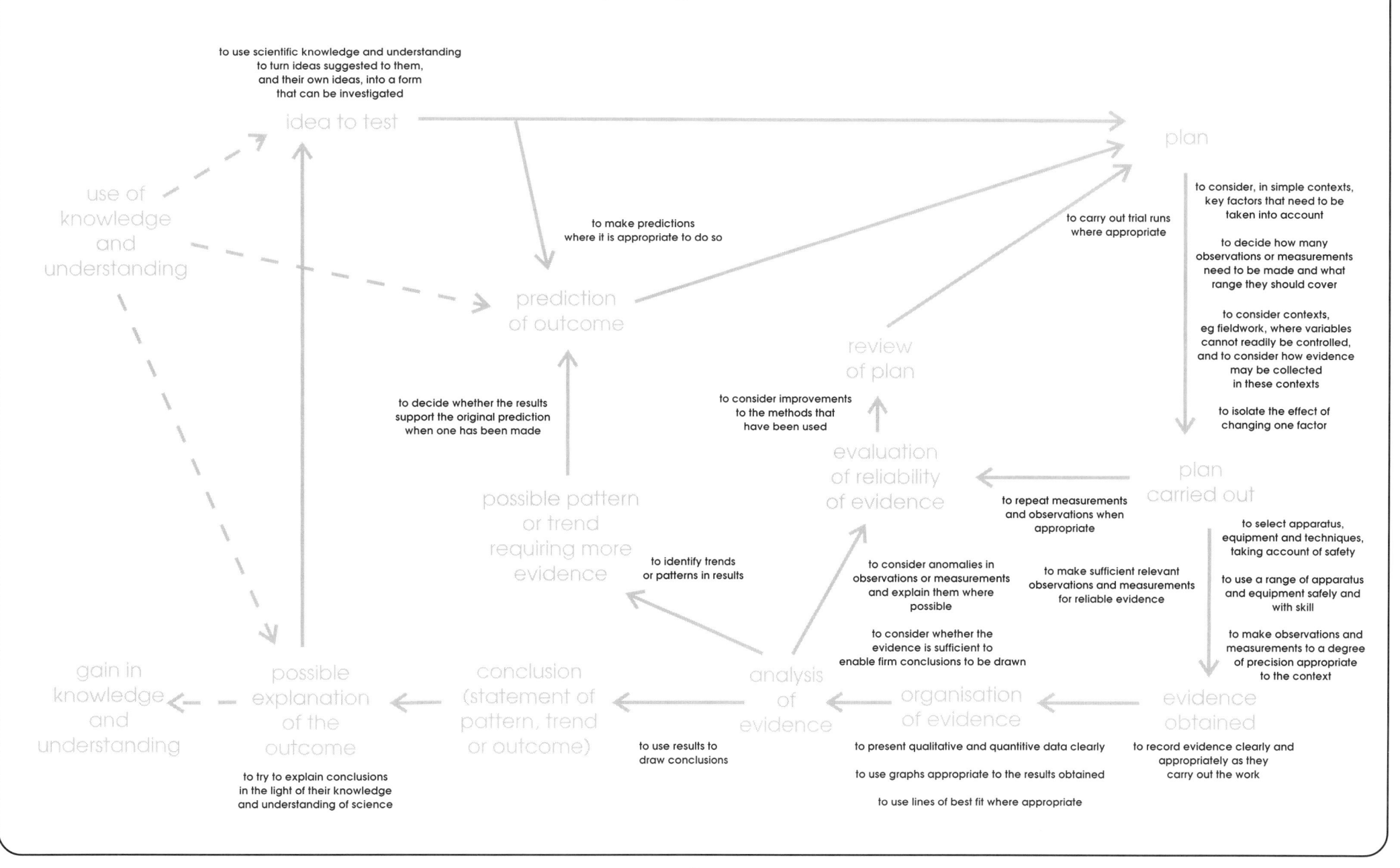

to use scientific knowledge and understanding to turn ideas suggested to them, and their own ideas, into a form that can be investigated

idea to test → **plan**

use of knowledge and understanding

to consider, in simple contexts, key factors that need to be taken into account

to make predictions where it is appropriate to do so

to carry out trial runs where appropriate

to decide how many observations or measurements need to be made and what range they should cover

prediction of outcome

to consider contexts, eg fieldwork, where variables cannot readily be controlled, and to consider how evidence may be collected in these contexts

review of plan

to isolate the effect of changing one factor

to decide whether the results support the original prediction when one has been made

to consider improvements to the methods that have been used

plan carried out

evaluation of reliability of evidence

to repeat measurements and observations when appropriate

to select apparatus, equipment and techniques, taking account of safety

possible pattern or trend requiring more evidence

to identify trends or patterns in results

to consider anomalies in observations or measurements and explain them where possible

to make sufficient relevant observations and measurements for reliable evidence

to use a range of apparatus and equipment safely and with skill

to consider whether the evidence is sufficient to enable firm conclusions to be drawn

to make observations and measurements to a degree of precision appropriate to the context

gain in knowledge and understanding ← **possible explanation of the outcome** ← **conclusion (statement of pattern, trend or outcome)** ← **analysis of evidence** ← **organisation of evidence** ← **evidence obtained**

to use results to draw conclusions

to present qualitative and quantitive data clearly

to record evidence clearly and appropriately as they carry out the work

to try to explain conclusions in the light of their knowledge and understanding of science

to use graphs appropriate to the results obtained

to use lines of best fit where appropriate

13

How the Scientific Process Fits the Programme of Study for Sc1
Key Stage Four

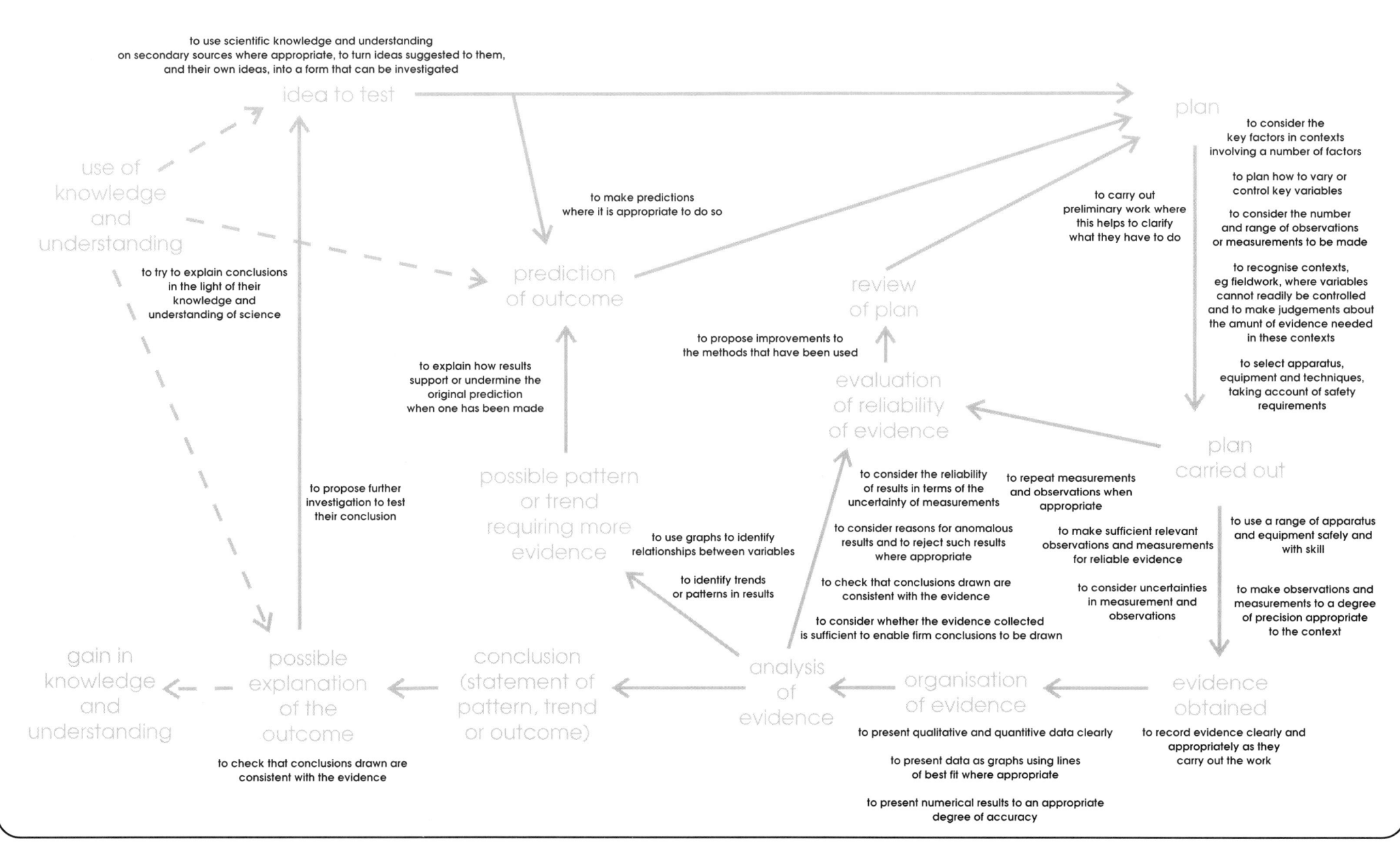

use of knowledge and understanding

to use scientific knowledge and understanding on secondary sources where appropriate, to turn ideas suggested to them, and their own ideas, into a form that can be investigated

idea to test

plan

to consider the key factors in contexts involving a number of factors

to plan how to vary or control key variables

to make predictions where it is appropriate to do so

to carry out preliminary work where this helps to clarify what they have to do

to consider the number and range of observations or measurements to be made

to try to explain conclusions in the light of their knowledge and understanding of science

prediction of outcome

review of plan

to recognise contexts, eg fieldwork, where variables cannot readily be controlled and to make judgements about the amount of evidence needed in these contexts

to propose improvements to the methods that have been used

to select apparatus, equipment and techniques, taking account of safety requirements

to explain how results support or undermine the original prediction when one has been made

evaluation of reliability of evidence

plan carried out

possible pattern or trend requiring more evidence

to consider the reliability of results in terms of the uncertainty of measurements

to repeat measurements and observations when appropriate

to propose further investigation to test their conclusion

to consider reasons for anomalous results and to reject such results where appropriate

to make sufficient relevant observations and measurements for reliable evidence

to use a range of apparatus and equipment safely and with skill

to use graphs to identify relationships between variables

to identify trends or patterns in results

to check that conclusions drawn are consistent with the evidence

to consider uncertainties in measurement and observations

to make observations and measurements to a degree of precision appropriate to the context

to consider whether the evidence collected is sufficient to enable firm conclusions to be drawn

gain in knowledge and understanding ← **possible explanation of the outcome** ← **conclusion (statement of pattern, trend or outcome)** ← **analysis of evidence** ← **organisation of evidence** ← **evidence obtained**

to present qualitative and quantitive data clearly

to record evidence clearly and appropriately as they carry out the work

to check that conclusions drawn are consistent with the evidence

to present data as graphs using lines of best fit where appropriate

to present numerical results to an appropriate degree of accuracy

Chapter 2

Experimental and Investigative Science Exemplified

page   16   The Teacher Decides
              17   Examples of the Experimental and Investigative Science Continuum
              24   The Flexibility of the Scientific Process

The Teacher Decides

The way in which the scientific process cycle operates is illustrated in this chapter by exemplifying four different approaches to the whole process as it occurs in the classroom across the Experimental and Investigative Science continuum. The teacher will decide which of these approaches most appropriately supports the learning of knowledge and understanding as well as choosing the best context for the practical activity.

When generating learning objectives, the teacher will determine whether children will mostly gain knowledge and understanding from the practical activity or use knowledge and understanding to support ideas and predictions.

The teacher may also decide to have different entry points into the scientific process cycle. Decisions of this nature during curriculum planning will enable teachers to achieve a greater balance in the teaching of all aspects of the cycle. Practical work requiring different levels of complexity in carrying out experimental procedures, data collection or analysis of evidence enables appropriate emphasis to be placed upon more demanding learning objectives.

The practical activities in this chapter are intended to help readers understand the breadth and depth available within Experimental and Investigative Science.

They demonstrate:

- examples of the Experimental and Investigative Science continuum
- different classroom management strategies
- the different skills and processes being used in practical activities
- different entry and exit points possible within the scientific process cycle
- the continuity and consistency across the key stages
- progression in complexity of the whole scientific process
- progression in complexity of specific aspects of the scientific process

The Experimental and Investigative Science Continuum
Children Following Instructions Provided by the Teacher

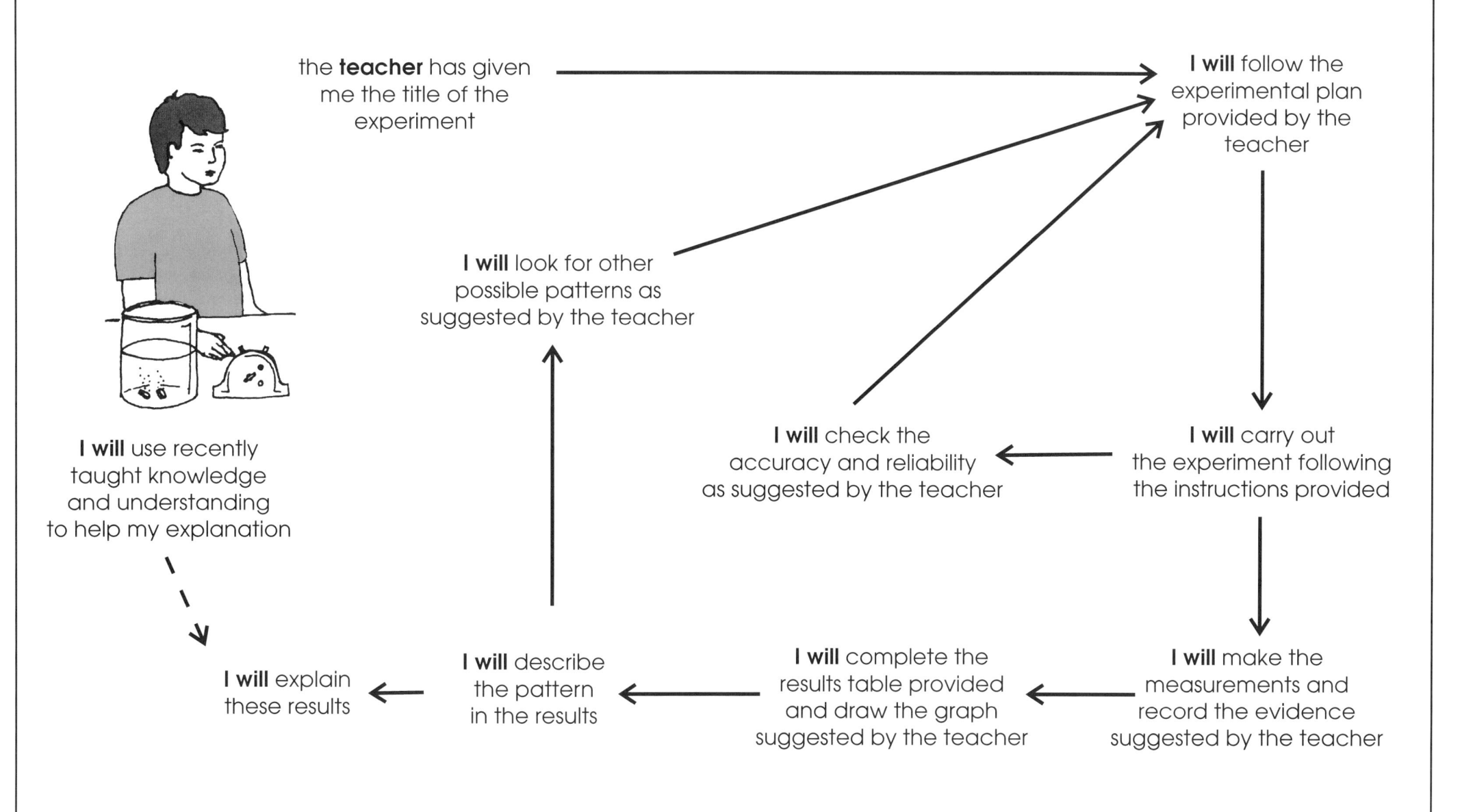

- the **teacher** has given me the title of the experiment
- **I will** follow the experimental plan provided by the teacher
- **I will** look for other possible patterns as suggested by the teacher
- **I will** check the accuracy and reliability as suggested by the teacher
- **I will** carry out the experiment following the instructions provided
- **I will** make the measurements and record the evidence suggested by the teacher
- **I will** complete the results table provided and draw the graph suggested by the teacher
- **I will** describe the pattern in the results
- **I will** explain these results
- **I will** use recently taught knowledge and understanding to help my explanation

The Experimental and Investigative Science Continuum
Teacher Demonstration Followed by Analysis of Evidence by the Children

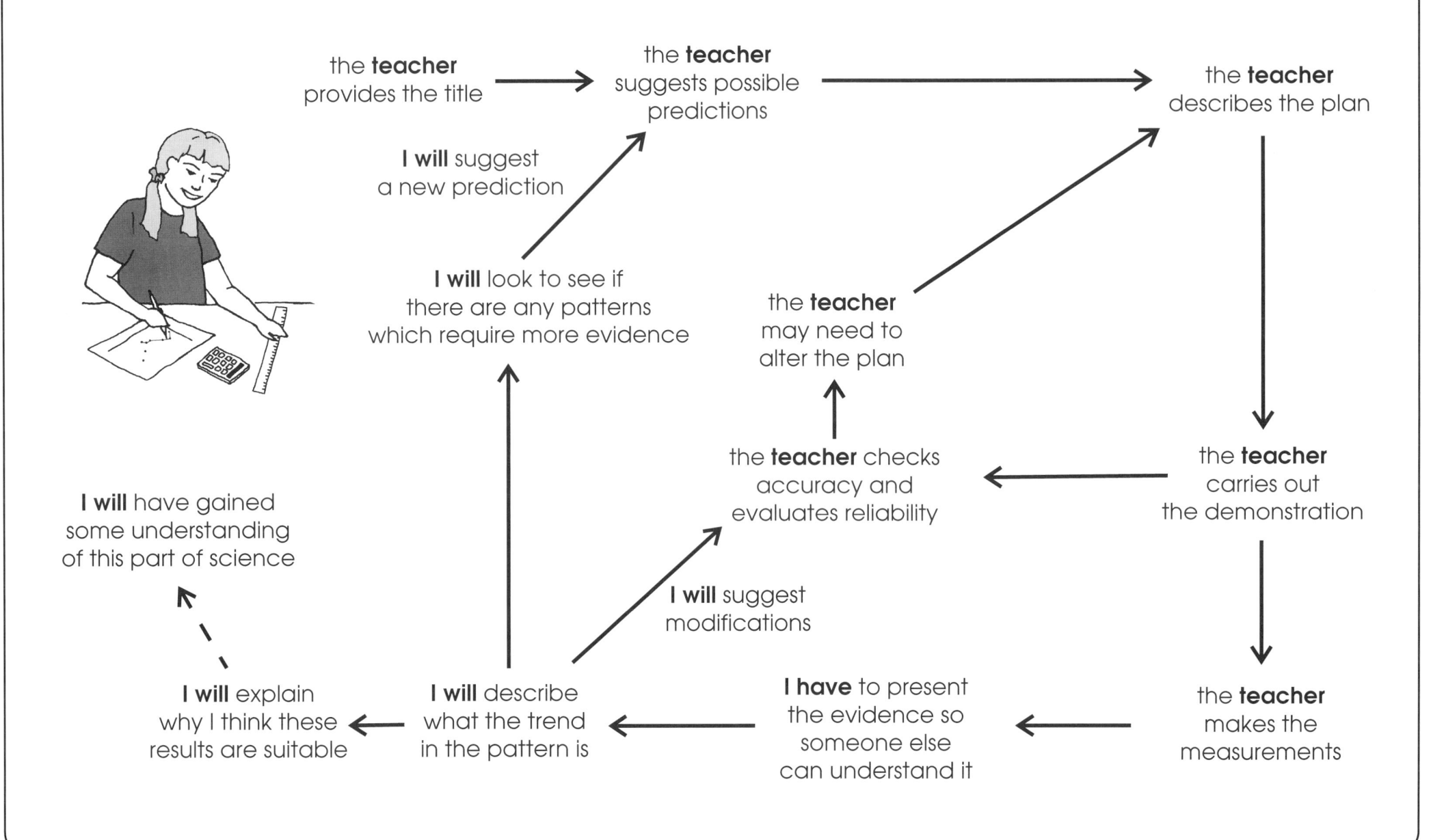

the **teacher** provides the title → the **teacher** suggests possible predictions → the **teacher** describes the plan

I will suggest a new prediction

I will look to see if there are any patterns which require more evidence

the **teacher** may need to alter the plan

the **teacher** checks accuracy and evaluates reliability

the **teacher** carries out the demonstration

I will suggest modifications

I will have gained some understanding of this part of science

I will explain why I think these results are suitable ← **I will** describe what the trend in the pattern is ← **I have** to present the evidence so someone else can understand it ← the **teacher** makes the measurements

The Experimental and Investigative Science Continuum
Class/Group Practical Activity, but Individual Children Predict, Plan and Carry Out

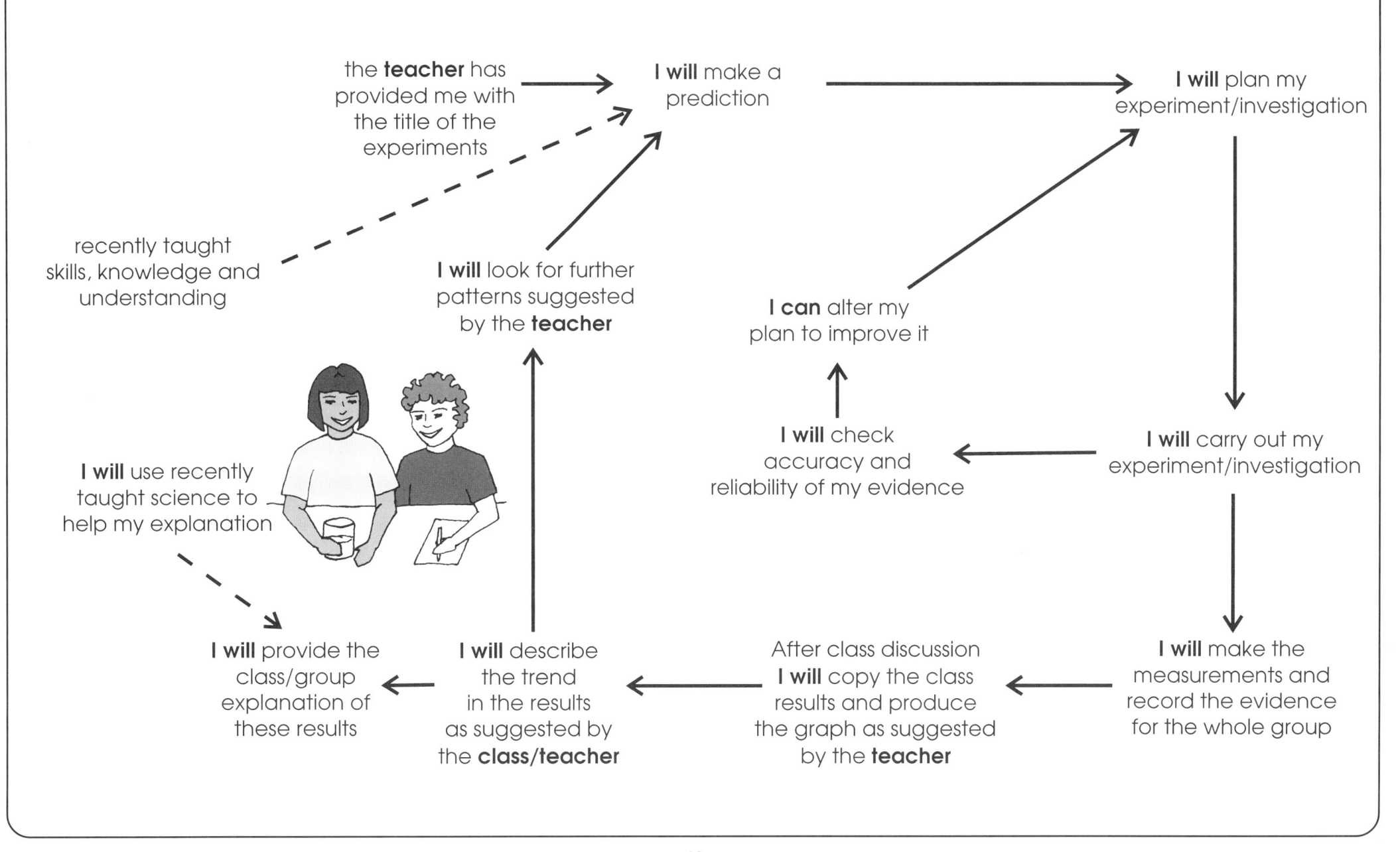

- the **teacher** has provided me with the title of the experiments
- **I will** make a prediction
- **I will** plan my experiment/investigation
- recently taught skills, knowledge and understanding
- **I will** look for further patterns suggested by the **teacher**
- **I can** alter my plan to improve it
- **I will** check accuracy and reliability of my evidence
- **I will** carry out my experiment/investigation
- **I will** use recently taught science to help my explanation
- **I will** provide the class/group explanation of these results
- **I will** describe the trend in the results as suggested by the **class/teacher**
- After class discussion **I will** copy the class results and produce the graph as suggested by the **teacher**
- **I will** make the measurements and record the evidence for the whole group

The Experimental and Investigative Science Continuum
A Whole Investigation Completed by the Children

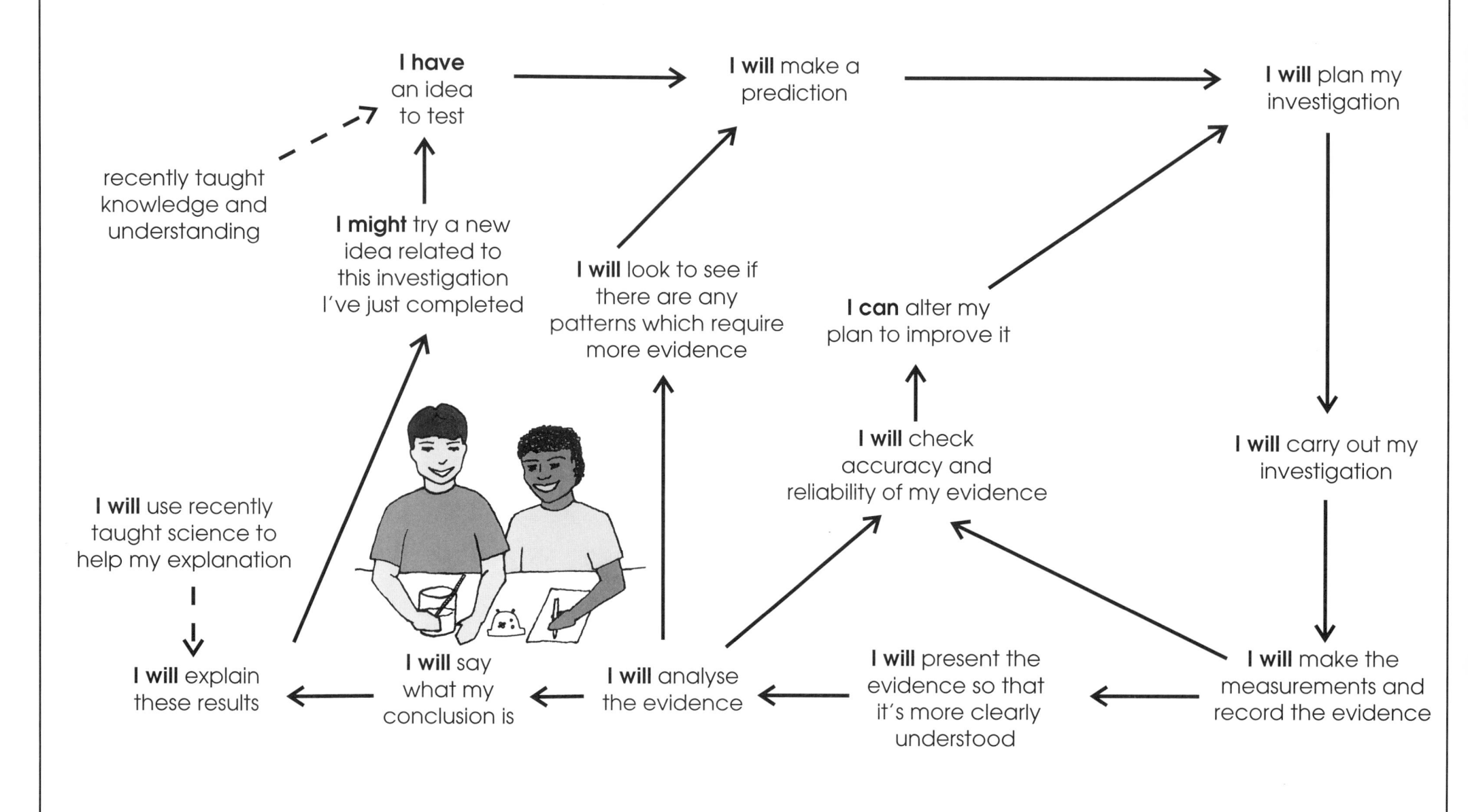

- **I have** an idea to test
- **I will** make a prediction
- **I will** plan my investigation
- recently taught knowledge and understanding
- **I might** try a new idea related to this investigation I've just completed
- **I will** look to see if there are any patterns which require more evidence
- **I can** alter my plan to improve it
- **I will** check accuracy and reliability of my evidence
- **I will** carry out my investigation
- **I will** use recently taught science to help my explanation
- **I will** explain these results
- **I will** say what my conclusion is
- **I will** analyse the evidence
- **I will** present the evidence so that it's more clearly understood
- **I will** make the measurements and record the evidence

Different Starting Points - Which May Be Used by the Teacher

All of the examples provided so far show that the teacher has decided to utilise all parts of the scientific process. The teacher may, however, decide that there are occasions when he/she wishes to start the scientific process at a different part of the cycle. The next three pages illustrate how this might take place.

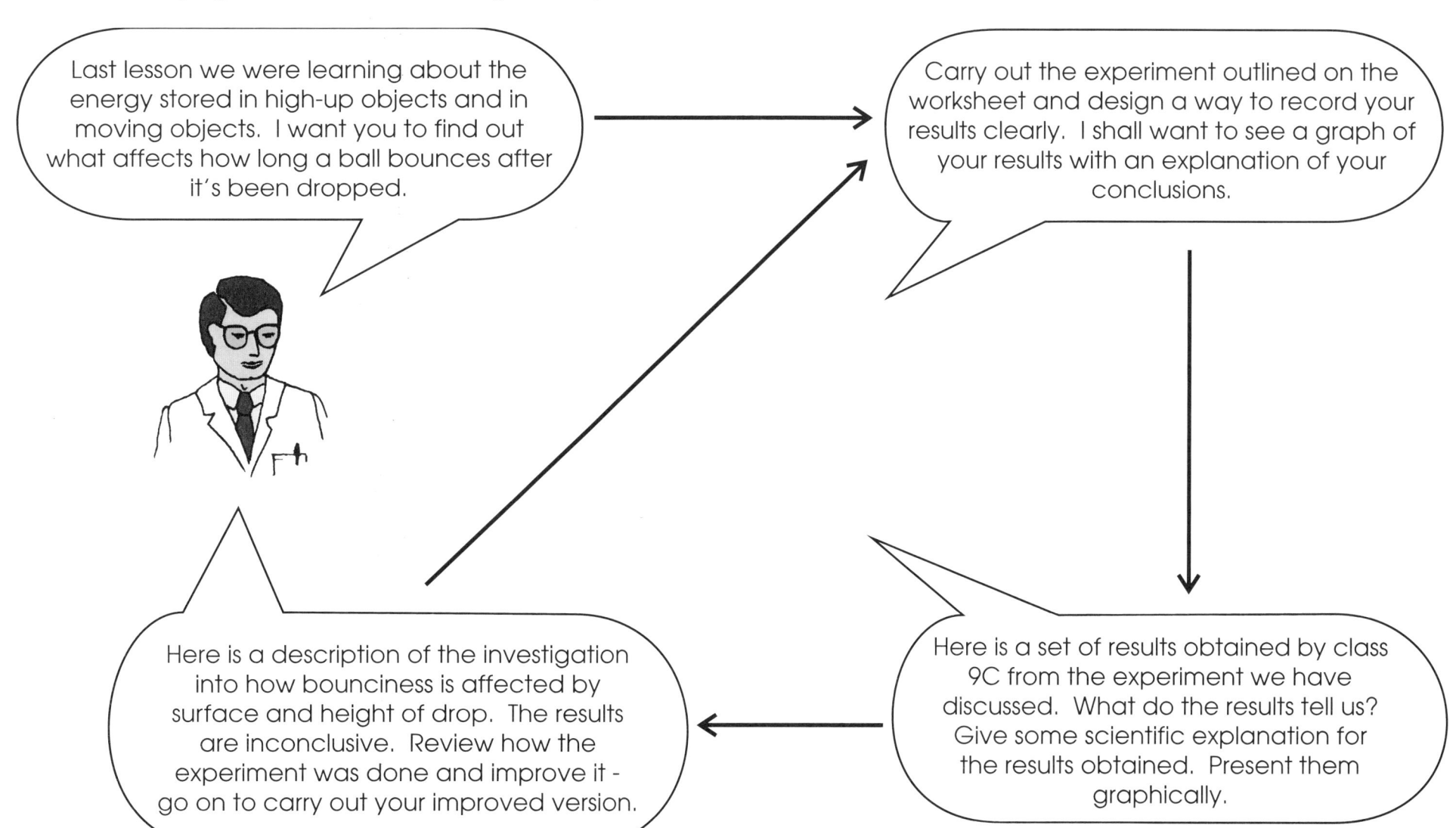

Top-left speech bubble: "Last lesson we were learning about the energy stored in high-up objects and in moving objects. I want you to find out what affects how long a ball bounces after it's been dropped."

Top-right speech bubble: "Carry out the experiment outlined on the worksheet and design a way to record your results clearly. I shall want to see a graph of your results with an explanation of your conclusions."

Bottom-right speech bubble: "Here is a set of results obtained by class 9C from the experiment we have discussed. What do the results tell us? Give some scientific explanation for the results obtained. Present them graphically."

Bottom-left speech bubble: "Here is a description of the investigation into how bounciness is affected by surface and height of drop. The results are inconclusive. Review how the experiment was done and improve it - go on to carry out your improved version."

Two possible Starting Points for an Investigation at Key Stage 1

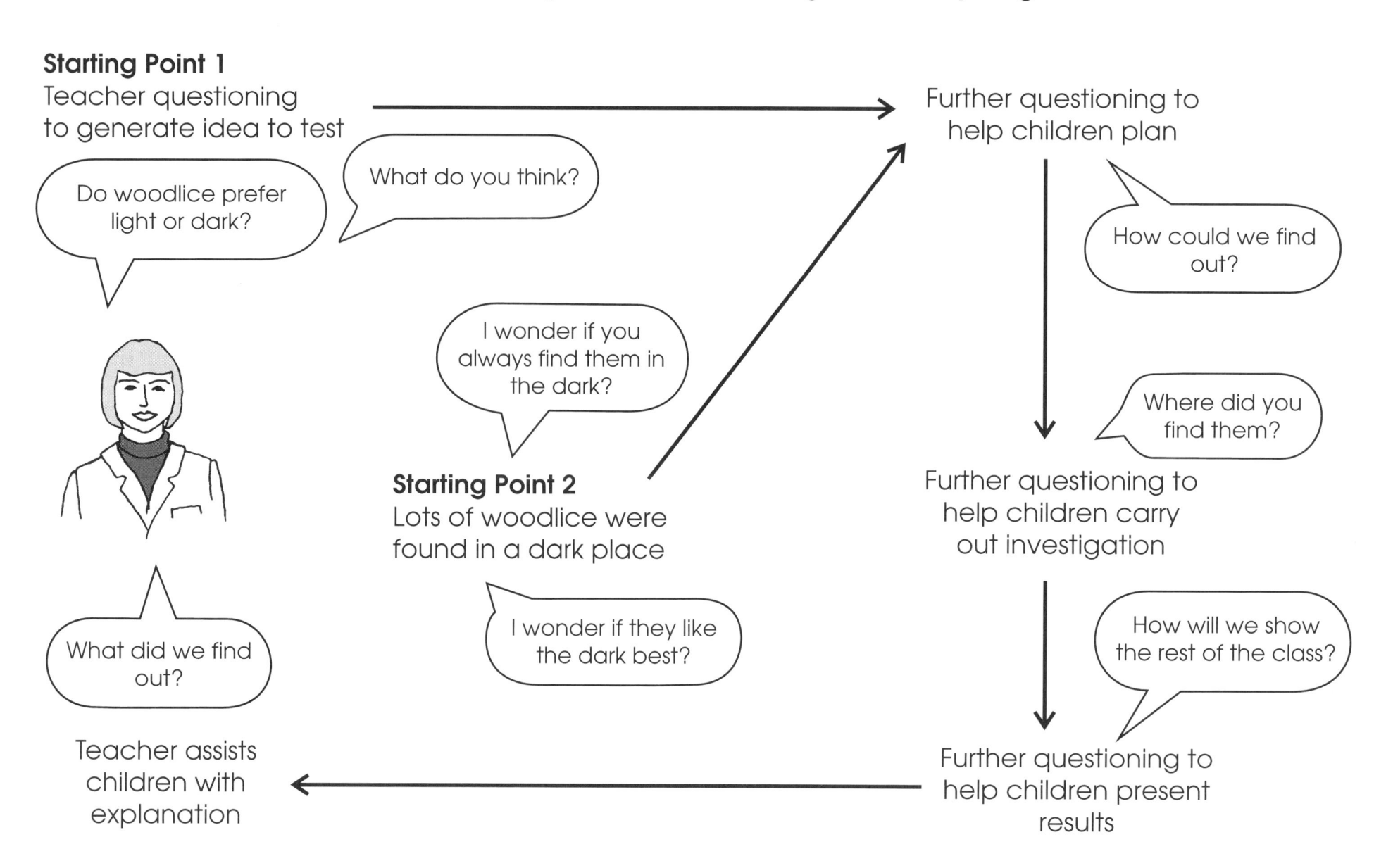

Starting Point 1
Teacher questioning to generate idea to test

Do woodlice prefer light or dark?

What do you think?

Starting Point 2
Lots of woodlice were found in a dark place

I wonder if you always find them in the dark?

I wonder if they like the dark best?

Further questioning to help children plan

How could we find out?

Where did you find them?

Further questioning to help children carry out investigation

How will we show the rest of the class?

Further questioning to help children present results

What did we find out?

Teacher assists children with explanation

Five Possible Starting Points for an Investigation at Key Stage 3

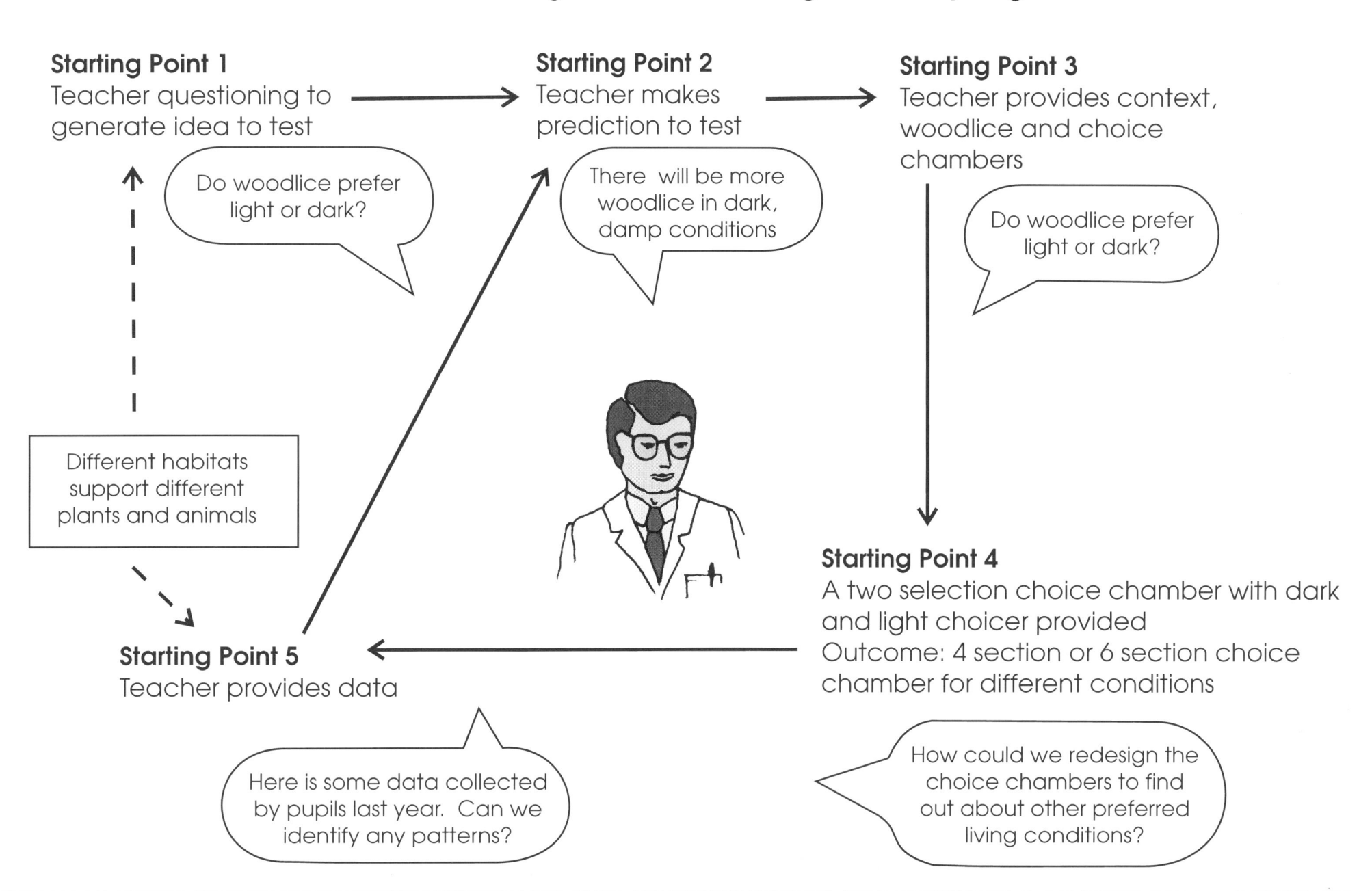

Starting Point 1
Teacher questioning to generate idea to test

Do woodlice prefer light or dark?

Starting Point 2
Teacher makes prediction to test

There will be more woodlice in dark, damp conditions

Starting Point 3
Teacher provides context, woodlice and choice chambers

Do woodlice prefer light or dark?

Different habitats support different plants and animals

Starting Point 4
A two selection choice chamber with dark and light choicer provided
Outcome: 4 section or 6 section choice chamber for different conditions

How could we redesign the choice chambers to find out about other preferred living conditions?

Starting Point 5
Teacher provides data

Here is some data collected by pupils last year. Can we identify any patterns?

The Flexibility of the Scientific Process

The key feature of this chapter is how teachers make use of the cyclical scientific process in the classroom.

During planning teachers will use the scientific process to review all the practical activities in a scheme of work. Decisions will be made about whether the activity is heavily directed experimental work or totally independent investigative work or somewhere between these two extremes along the continuum (see page 2).

The progression in Sc1 can be implemented (see chapter 3) so that the development of skills and processes can take place within and across the key stages. Decisions about whether it is appropriate to base a piece of practical activity on prior scientific knowledge and understanding or whether skills and processes only will be developed can also be made.

The management issues of each selected practical activity will be identified, ie will the whole scientific process be needed or will it be appropriate to select daily part of the process? Decisions about which practical activities are to be used for the assessment of Sc1 and which children will be assessed can also be made.

However, it will be the teacher who decides how the scientific process occurs in the classroom.

The teacher will decide whether to:

- provide the children with detailed or partial instructions

- undertake a demonstration of part of the scientific process allowing the children to complete the other aspects themselves

- manage whole class or group practical activities where children co-operatively or individually predict, plan and carry out

- manage whole investigations where children work individually or co-operatively

- have different entry points into the scientific process

or

- mix and match any of the above so that the selected approach most appropriately suits the learning objective of the practical activity

Chapter 3

Progression in Experimental and Investigative Science

page 26 Progression in Experimental and Investigative Science
        27 Progression in Context and Scale
        30 Lines of Progression
        32 Lines of Progression in Planning
        34 Lines of Progression in Obtaining Evidence
        36 Lines of Progression in Considering Evidence
        38 Summative Assessment

Progression in Experimental and Investigative Science

Children's abilities to investigate develop from relatively simple beginnings in the early years through to more sophisticated levels as teenagers. Progression in a number of aspects of experimental work can be charted as children mature and develop. Using the 1995 Orders for science and SCAA exemplification publications we have mapped out progression in three main areas of experimental and investigative work. These relate directly to the three sub-headings of Sc1 at key stages 1 and 2. The third and fourth sub-headings of Sc1 at key stages 3 and 4 (considering the strength of evidence, analysing evidence and drawing conclusions) are accounted for in the "considering evidence" area of experimental and investigative work.

- planning
- obtaining evidence
- considering evidence

Each of these has been sub-divided to give nine lines of progression.

planning

- considering factors and fair testing - including manipulation of variables
- resources - selecting appropriate equipment
- predicting

obtaining evidence

- context and scale - the range and sophistication of investigations carried out
- using equipment
- observing and measuring - the degree of accuracy with which equipment is used

considering evidence

- organising evidence - organising into tables, graphs etc
- analysing and explaining - including drawing conclusions
- evaluating - reliability and validity of methods and evidence

Progression in Context and Scale

As children progress, the complexity of their investigations and the range of contexts in which they carry them out increase. This is the way in which all of the lines of progression operate. This increasing scale of complexity and range of contexts in which pupils can operate is illustrated on pages 28 and 29. This illustration is an interpretation of the scale and contexts contained within the level descriptions for Sc1. It is important that this progression is seen as the framework within which the lines of progression are set. Although context and scale is not really a single line of progression, rather an overlay of sophistication affecting all the lines of progression on pages 32 to 37, it has been summarised as a single line of progression within the obtaining evidence area. This is an over-simplification but one that makes it easier for the user to have a convenient summary.

Example Line of Progression

context and scale	simple one stage tasks	simple tasks with several stages, to find out something	simple tests to find something out, often a fair test	can carry out fair tests in context of Sc2, 3 or 4, involving the effect of one main factor	carry out investigations involving just a few factors	carry out investigations involving several factors	confidently carry out investigations possibly involving several factors in contexts from Sc2, 3 and 4	able to take a strategic view of complex investigations and carry them out across a wide range of contexts using appropriate strategies	confidently carry out more complex investigations across a wide range of contexts, including those which are outside their direct experience
type of practical work which illustrated the level of complexity	looking at the leaves from different trees	testing to find out which powders dissolve in water and which don't	comparing which of 6 rocks absorb most water, counting out similar sized water drops	does the surface affect the force needed to pull a wooden block along?	finding out what affects the strength of an electromagnet (changing the number of turns whilst retaining the core and controlling a constant current)	which is the best antacid remedy? (testing 6 remedies and measuring the volume of acid neutralised; controlling the mass of powder used, hydrochloric acid concentration, and considering whether time, stirring and temperature are important)	what conditions are best for the digestion of starch? (able to consider both the effect of pH and temperature; controlling the amounts of starch and amylase used)	investigating the effect of concentration of acid on reaction with marble chips by the mass loss from the flask and correlating with the rate of carbon dioxide production can organise a long term investigation by appropriate data logging	investigating the links between water hardness and mineral content (researching background information and carrying out titrations using dilute soap solution)
based upon level description	1	2	3	4	5	6	7	8	exceptional performance

Illustrating the Progression in Context and Scale

context and scale	simple one stage tasks	simple tasks with several stages, to find out something	simple tests to find something out, often a fair test	can carry out fair tests in context of Sc2, 3 or 4, involving the effect of one main factor	carry out investigations involving just a few factors
type of practical work which illustrated the level of complexity	looking at the leaves from different trees	testing to find out which powders dissolve in water and which don't	comparing which of 6 rocks absorb most water, counting out similar sized water drops	does the surface affect the force needed to pull a wooden block along?	finding out what affects the strength of an electromagnet (changing the number of turns whilst retaining the core and controlling a constant current)
based upon level description	1	2	3	4	5

carry out investigations involving several factors	confidently carry out investigations possibly involving several factors in contexts from Sc2, 3 and 4	able to take a strategic view of complex investigations and carry them out across a wide range of contexts using appropriate strategies	confidently carry out more complex investigations across a wide range of contexts, including those which are outside their direct experience
which is the best antacid remedy? (testing 6 remedies and measuring the volume of acid neutralised; controlling the mass of powder used, hydrochloric acid concentration, and considering whether time, stirring and temperature are important)	what conditions are best for the digestion of starch? (able to consider both the effect of pH and temperature; controlling the amounts of starch and amylase used)	investigating the effect of concentration of acid on reaction with marble chips by the mass loss from the flask and correlating with the rate of carbon dioxide production can organise a long term investigation by appropriate data logging	investigating the links between water hardness and mineral content (researching background information and carrying out titrations using dilute soap solution)
6	7	8	exceptional performance

Lines of Progression

These lines of progression are presented across the page as a series of steps. It is intended that each step subsumes the previous step but it should not be assumed that each is of equivalent difficulty. They have only been set out as regular spaces on the page for the convenience of the user. The steps in the nine lines of progression do not necessarily match each other in exact level of difficulty, nor do they reach the same heights - some, such as resourcing, 'plateau' at intermediate levels. In such cases further progression can come from applying that skill in increasingly wider or more demanding contexts.

Each of the nine points along the lines of progression has been numbered to reflect the level description for Experimental and Investigative Science with which it is associated. These levels are attached for guidance only; they are not definitive. Lines of progression should not be used for crude mathematical aggregation in order to produce end of key stage teacher assessments.

Using Lines of Progression in Teaching and Learning

The lines of progression have a number of functions in the teaching of science

- informing long, medium and short term planning
- formative assessment
- pupil self-assessment
- contributing to summative assessment

Informing Long and Medium Term Planning

Long and medium planning enables the selection and allocation of practical work to key stages and within a key stage or a particular year group. Lines of progression can be used to review across the key stage or across consecutive key stages to ensure that year on year pupils are meeting successively more challenging experimental and investigative work and encountering a wider range of contexts in which it is set. Lines of progression can also be used to review schemes of work to ensure that across each year there are sufficient opportunities to cover all aspects of practical work at depths appropriate to the age, experience and abilities of the pupils in the class. Not all practical tasks will offer potential for all aspects of investigation; for example many investigations do not require the child to make a prediction. A prediction is not compulsory, in many circumstances it will not be appropriate. Therefore a range of activities needs to be planned so that children have sufficient opportunities to develop in all aspects of experimental investigation work.

Formative Assessment

Lines of progression provide a comprehensive framework with a large number of possible bench marks against which individual children's progress can be measured. They can be used in a more developmental way by matching a child's achievement against the points on the lines of progression and identifying possible areas of weakness or helping to determine the next step in learning, ie informing short term planning. "Indicators of levelness" for each practical activity could be produced and examples of these can be found in Chapter 9 "How Can We Recognise Attainment in Sc1?"

Short Term Planning

On a lesson-by-lesson basis it is necessary to plan or adjust existing plans, so that children experience activities appropriate to their current learning. Identifying the next step along the line of progression will help determine the future learning objectives for practical science and thus the plan for following lessons. "Some Possible Milestones - Assessment Sc1" on pages 102 and 103 will help teachers to identify children's understanding of the scientific process during lessons.

Lines of progression are used to ensure...

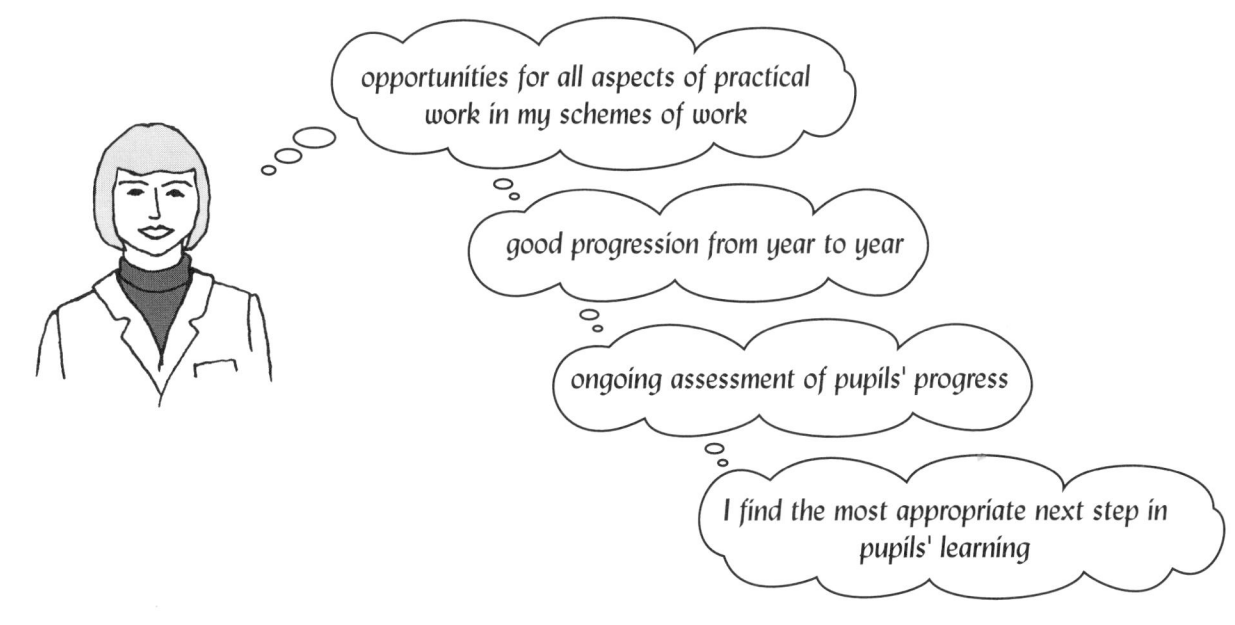

- *opportunities for all aspects of practical work in my schemes of work*
- *good progression from year to year*
- *ongoing assessment of pupils' progress*
- *I find the most appropriate next step in pupils' learning*

Lines of Progression in Planning

considering factors and fair testing

knows what to do after discussion with adult, but unable to make useful suggestions	suggest some ways of finding things out when helped	suggest ways of finding things out carry out a fair test with help	plan an investigation showing understanding of the need for a fair test carry out a fair test with help	confidently identify all the key factors in experiments and investigations involving only a few factors

resourcing

discusses equipment with teacher but unable to make decision about possible equipment	suggest some equipment needed when helped	make independent suggestions for what equipment may be required	plan what equipment will be needed for simple tasks and tests	consistently plan what equipment is needed for more sophisticated tasks such as experiments and investigations

predicting

are unaware of any probable outcomes of a task	think about what is expected to happen in a simple task	make simple predictions where outcomes are relatively obvious	make predictions which are reasoned but not yet explicit	make predictions which are explicit and may be based on scientific knowledge
1	2	3	4	5

use scientific knowledge and understanding to identify the key factors	use scientific knowledge and understanding to identify the key factors from amongst many, some of which it may not be possible to control	recognise that different types of experimental work require different approaches use scientific knowledge and understanding to identify a strategy for an investigation (and the key factors from amongst many)	use additional information from various sources to help plan a strategy
plan the use of equipment to give appropriately accurate results in investigations	plan and resource investigations in accordance with increasing range of contexts and scale	plan and resource investigations in accordance with increasing range of contexts and scale	plan and resource investigations in accordance with increasing range of contexts and scale
use scientific knowledge and understanding to predict the effect of the input variable/factor on the outcome use scientific knowledge and understanding to make further predictions based on patterns in their results	use scientific knowledge and understanding to make predictions appropriate to the increasing range of contexts and scale	use scientific knowledge and understanding to make predictions appropriate to the increasing range of contexts and scale	use detailed scientific knowledge and understanding to make predictions appropriate to the increasing range of contexts and scale
6	**7**	**8**	**exceptional performance**

Lines of Progress in Obtaining Evidence

context and scale

carry out simple one stage tasks	carry out simple tasks, often suggested to them (but, as yet, has no clear notion of a fair test)	carry out simple tests, often fair test	carry out simple fair tests involving the effect of one main factor	carry out investigations involving just a few factors

using equipment

use basic equipment under instruction	use simple equipment to achieve a result, such as hand lens or measuring jug	select relevant equipment such as metre rule, scales or thermometers	select appropriate apparatus routinely for a range of tasks use apparatus with care

observing and measuring

observe and describe simple features of objects, living things and events, using sight and/or other senses	make observations and simple comparisons	make relevant observations and measurements using both standard and non-standard units	make adequate observations and measurements for the task	repeat observations or measurements where there is obvious shortcoming or if prompted

| 1 | 2 | 3 | 4 | 5 |

confidently carry out investigations involving several factors	confidently carry out investigations involving several factors, across a range of contexts	take a strategic view of complex investigations and carry them out across a wide range of contexts using appropriate strategies	confidently carry out complex investigations across a wide range of contexts, including those which are outside their usual experience
select and use a wide range of apparatus, including that capable of measuring to fine divisions	use a wide range of apparatus with precision	manipulate apparatus with precision and skill	manipulate a wide range of apparatus with precision and skill in a wide variety of contexts
make a series of observations and measurements with appropriate precision make enough measurements or observations for the task	make systematic and precise observations and measurements identify particular areas where more data may be needed	decide on level of precision required and make measurements precise enough to test mathematical relationships decide which observations are relevant and omit irrelevant materials	observe and measure with the degree of selectivity and precision required by the wider range of contexts and demands
6	**7**	**8**	**exceptional performance**

Lines of Progression in Considering Evidence

(includes: 1 analysing evidence and drawing conclusions 2 considering the strength of evidence)

organising evidence

talk about what has been noticed use simple drawings or charts	describe observations clearly use simple tables	record observations with greater precision and detail, in a variety of ways	make clear presentations using tables and bar charts and plot very simple line graphs	record data systematically and represent information as line graphs when appropriate

analysing and explaining

describe and communicate findings	make comparisons between objects and events	describe where the findings may have been affected by the factor that was changed describe simple patterns in results say what has been found out	interpret tables, graphs etc to show trends use patterns to inform their conclusion begin to use scientific knowledge to help explain conclusions	draw conclusions consistent with evidence relate these to scientific knowledge when they are helped or where there is an obvious link

evaluating

accept whatever happens in a task without questioning it	say whether their findings are what they expected	recognise and say why a fair test is fair (or unfair)	identify factors and evidence which make a fair test	explain, with prompting why repeated (or average) measurements give greater reliability

| 1 | 2 | 3 | 4 | 5 |

record clearly and accurately draw line graphs with scales selected to effectively display the data	use line of best fit on graphs	draw graphs which allow for anomalous results, for example by drawing smooth curves which identify and ignore erroneous points	record precisely and concisely, focusing on matters of particular significance anomalous results are identified, dealt with and explained
explain their conclusions using scientific knowledge and understanding	explain their conclusions using scientific knowledge and understanding in a wide range of contexts recognise when clear patterns in evidence may not be sufficient to draw a full conclusion	draw conclusions which are consistent with the valid data, after it has been critically considered	use detailed scientific knowledge and understanding to draw conclusions from results, recognising and explaining salient features of the data consider whether or how to test their conclusions further
understand the need for sufficient reliable data identify data that do not fit the main pattern or trend	recognise uncertainty in measurements and where necessary repeats measurements and observations for greater reliability begin to consider whether data collected is sufficient for the conclusions drawn	identify relevant data by evaluating all the results gathered identify shortcomings and lack of precision in data tentatively offer explanations for anomalies	offer reasoned explanations for anomalous data give reasoned accounts of how they could collect any necessary additional data
6	**7**	**8**	**exceptional performance**

Summative Assessment

Pupil Self Assessment

By providing pupils with the lines of progression, simply worded, they can check their own progress in practical work and more clearly understand the objectives of the tasks being set. Examples of such simply worded statements can be found in Chapter 10, "How can we help children progress?", "In my practical science work I can...?" These will contribute to both formative and summative assessment.

Contributing to Summative Assessment

Records of pupils' achievements along lines of progression (possibly kept by the pupils themselves and validated by the teacher) could form the summative record of pupils' practical achievement at the end of the year or when pupils transfer between teachers.

At the end of a key stage a pupil's record of progress along the lines of progression could be used to guide the teacher towards the most appropriate level descriptions to consider in teacher assessment of Sc1. It is not intended that sheets be used for a crude arithmetic average level.

Summative Assessment at Key Stage 4

The examination boards in England and Wales have all agreed to use a common scheme of assessment. Four skill areas of Sc1 are identified and a number of statements (mark descriptions) have been provided.

Skill area 1:   Planning experimental procedures
Skill area 2:   Obtaining evidence
Skill area 3:   Analysing evidence and drawing conclusions
Skill area 4:   Evaluating evidence

Mark descriptions are provided for 2, 4, 6 and 8 marks in the first three skill areas and 2, 4 and 6 marks in the fourth skill area. Teachers will use professional judgement to decide which mark best fits the pupil's performance. There are no mark descriptions for 3, 5 and 7 marks. However, teachers will award these intermediate marks where performance exceeds one mark description and only partially satisfies the next.

The lines of progression have been cross referenced to the mark descriptions to ensure consistency with the requirements of the examination boards in England and Wales.

Chapter 4

What Are Factors or Variables?

page   40   What are Factors or Variables?
              42   Types of Variable
              43   Complexity of Variable
              45   How Factors and Variables Affect the Demand of Investigative Work

What are Factors or Variables?

Those aspects of an investigation which change, and can sometimes be controlled, are called factors or variables. Factors include those aspects which might change or have an effect on the investigation but cannot be directly controlled by the investigator, such as the westerly aspect of a building in an investigation into the weathering of building stone or the daily changes in light levels in an investigation into plant distribution near a copse.

Factors which can be directly controlled by the investigator are called variables. The factors outside the direct control of the investigator can still be included within the scope of the investigation; the investigator must take into account their possible effect on the investigation where necessary. In most investigations the word **factor** can be replaced by **variable**.

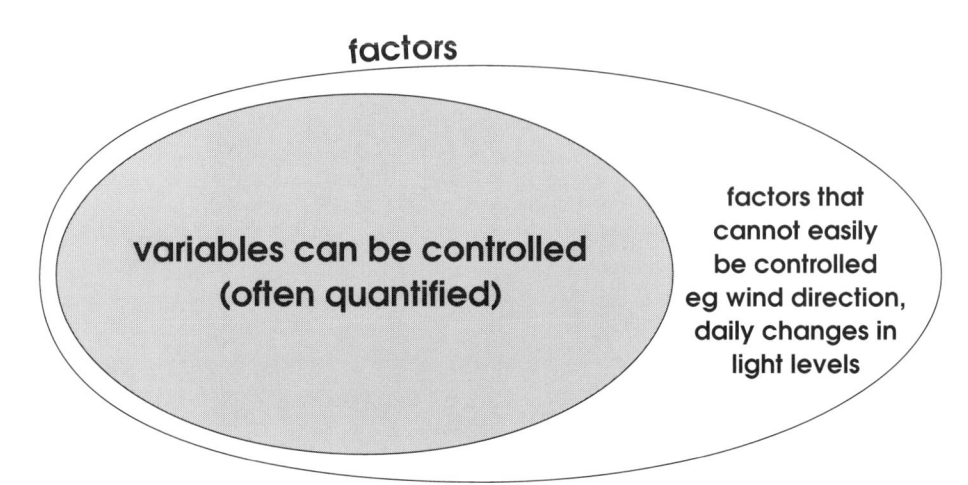

factors

variables can be controlled (often quantified)

factors that cannot easily be controlled eg wind direction, daily changes in light levels

It is useful to think of variables as belonging to one of three groups. All investigations, no matter how sophisticated, would have variables that can be assigned to these groups:

- variables we change deliberately
  input variables (also called independent variables)
- variables that change because we changed something else earlier
  outcome variables (also called dependent variables)
- variables we deliberately keep the same
  controlled variables (also called control variables)

Younger children, or those with special educational needs, may require help in identifying variables through direct teacher questioning such as, "Which things will you change?" or, "What things should you keep the same?" By the end of key stage 2 they should be able to use the terminology themselves in describing their investigation. During key stages 3 and 4 children will also begin to use more complicated terminology such as continuous, discrete and categoric variables.

Key Variables

The two variables that define the main parameters of an investigation are:

- **the input variable**
- **the outcome variable**

Therefore the input and outcome variables of an investigation are also referred to as the key variables.

The Variables in an Experiment or Investigation can be Classified in Several Ways

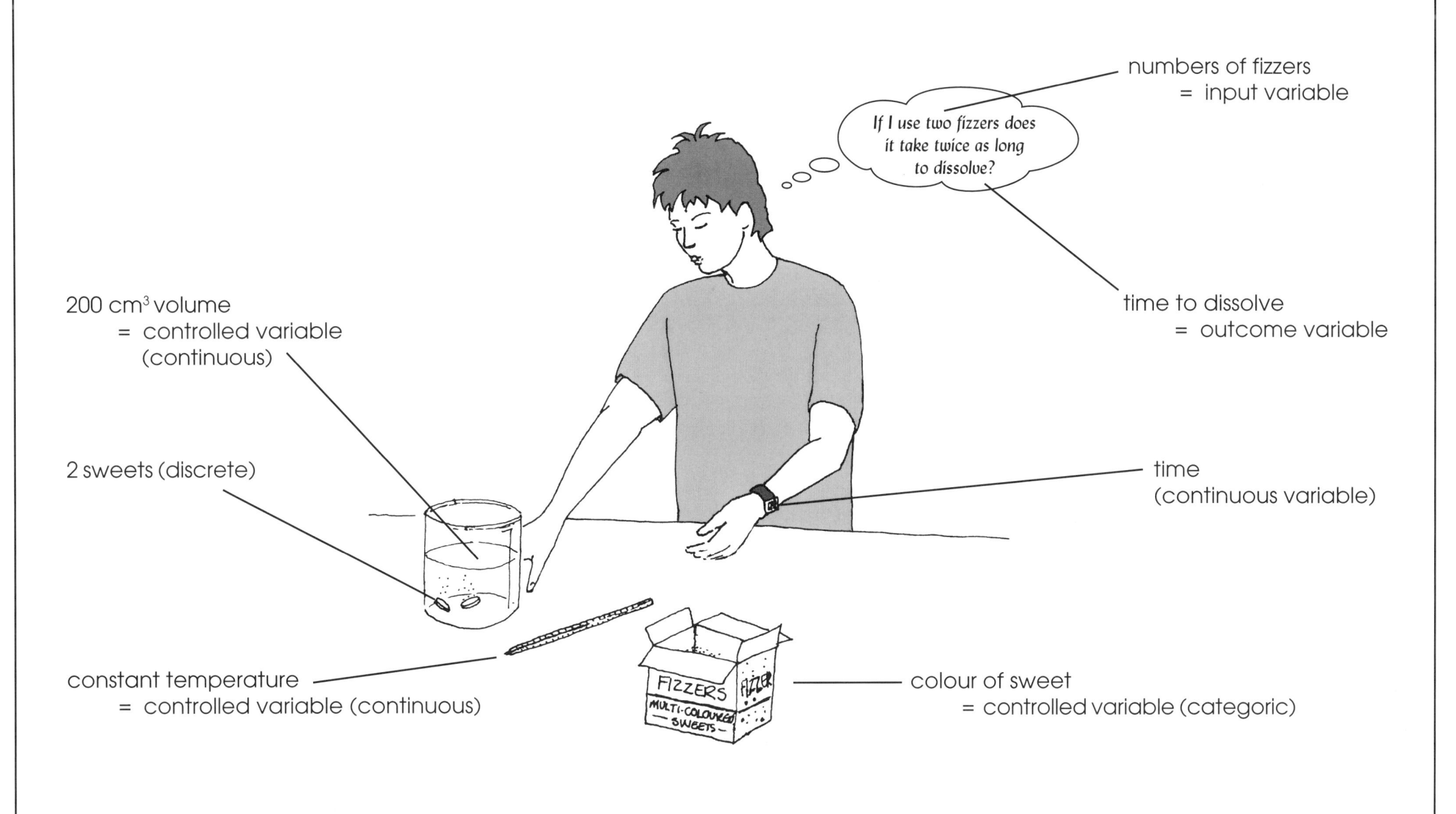

If I use two fizzers does it take twice as long to dissolve?

numbers of fizzers = input variable

time to dissolve = outcome variable

200 cm³ volume = controlled variable (continuous)

2 sweets (discrete)

time (continuous variable)

constant temperature = controlled variable (continuous)

colour of sweet = controlled variable (categoric)

FIZZERS — MULTI-COLOURED SWEETS

Types of Variable

Classed according to their function in the investigation

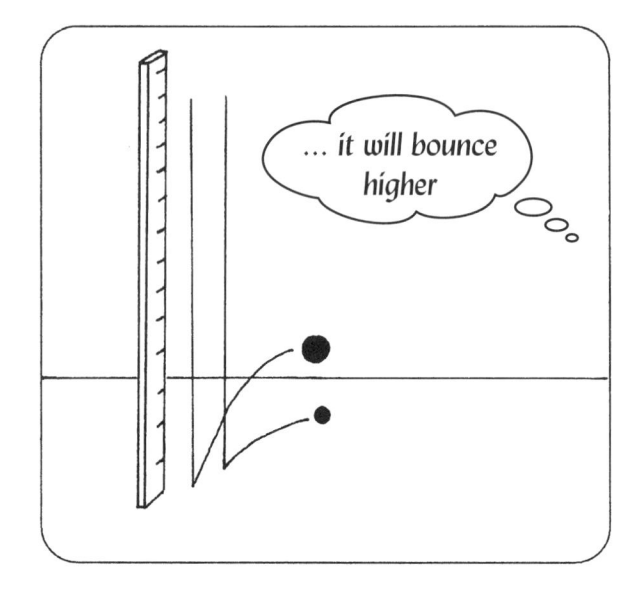

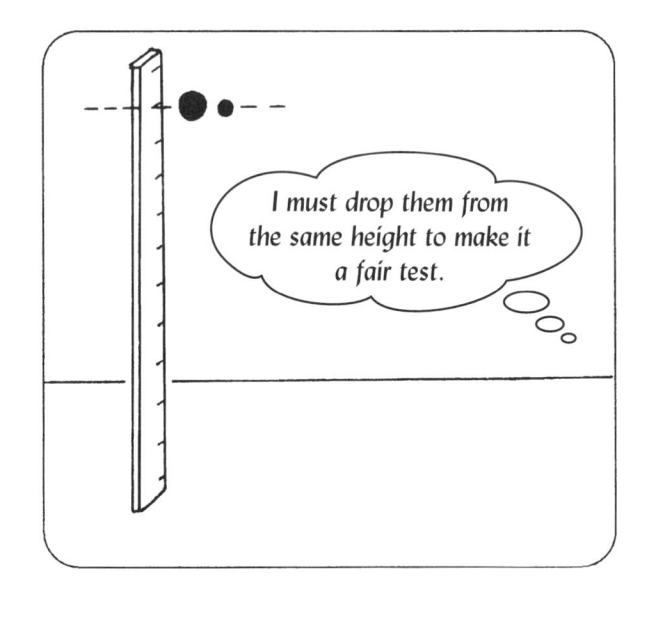

I predict that if the ball has twice the mass...

... it will bounce higher

I must drop them from the same height to make it a fair test.

Input Variable

(also called the **independent** variable) This is the factor you deliberately vary to find out what effect it has, in this case the mass of the ball.

Children find the word **input** less confusing than **independent**.

Outcome Variable

(also called the **dependent** variable) This is the factor that is affected by changing the input variable, in this case the height of the bounce.

Children find the word **outcome** less confusing than **dependent**.

Controlled Variable

(also called the **control** variable) These are the factors you have to keep the same to make it a fair test, in this case the height of the drop, the surface and the material of the balls.

Input and outcome variables are together called **key variables** of the investigation

Complexity of Variable

Classed according to sophistication of their measurement

Categoric Variable

This is a simple descriptive variable. It is assigned to a group, in this case colour.

No numerical values can be given to it. Hot/warm/cold and type of bird are other examples of categoric variable.

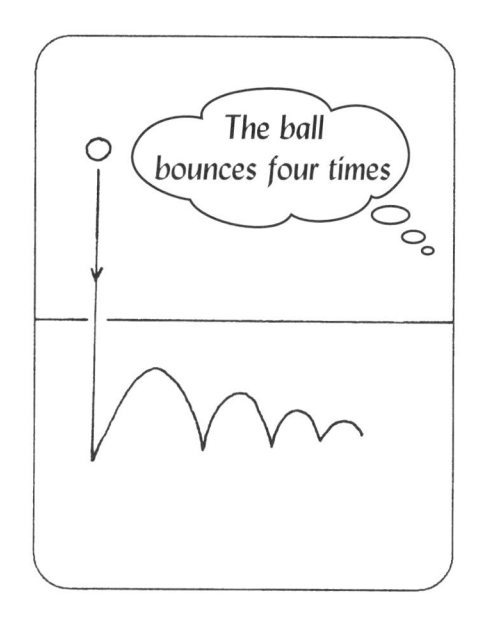

Discrete Variable

This is a variable that can have a whole number value, but not fractions or decimals, in this case 4 bounces. Number of legs, population and number of tablets are other examples of discrete variables. These are sometimes called discontinuous variables.

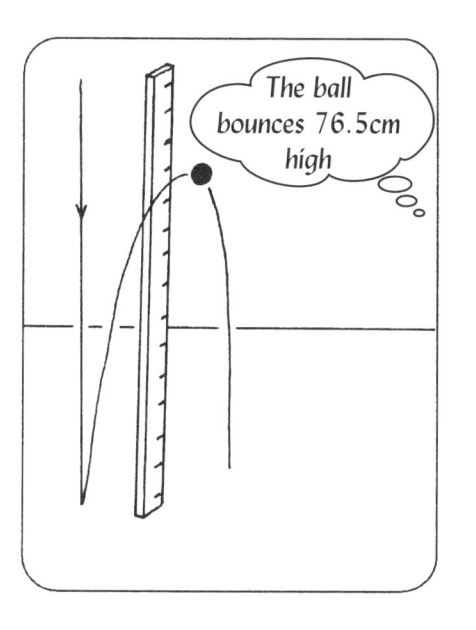

Continuous Variables

This is a variable that can take a numerical value anywhere along a continuum of numbers. It can be a decimal and does not have to be a whole number. In this case it is height in cm, but can be temperature, volume, mass, time etc.

Derived Variable

This is a variable that can be calculated from other variables which must first be measured. In this case, potential energy = mass x height x g. Velocity, acceleration, density and rate of reaction are all derived variables.

Complexity of Variable

Each type of variable - input, outcome, controlled - needs to be observed or measured. The degree of complexity of those measurements will vary according to the age and experience of the child and according to the demands of the investigation.

There are four classes of complexity of variables:

categoric   a variable assigned to a descriptive group, eg colour

discrete   a variable that can be measured in whole numbers, eg number of legs on a minibeast

continuous   a variable that can be measured by a range of numbers including fractions and decimals, eg the temperature is 18.5°C

derived   a variable that is calculated from the measurements of other variables, eg speed = 1.5 centimetres per second

Younger children will start investigating by using categoric variables and then discrete variables, whereas derived variables will be used more often in key stages 3 or 4. It is not necessary for children to know the names for these types of variable until they progress to higher levels of attainment.

descriptive - CATEGORIC
whole number - DISCRETE
decimal - CONTINUOUS
calculated - DERIVED

How Factors and Variables Affect the Demand of Investigative Learning

The number and complexity of variables used in practical work in part determines the level of experimental or investigative work achieved. On their own, the variables do not define the level of attainment but they may limit the level being achieved by a child. Where teachers clearly understand the nature of these factors they are able to encourage children to use the type of variables most appropriate and hence promote children's progress in Sc1. Teachers often do this by deciding which title best represents the desired outcomes of experimental or investigative work. So when they decide to include an investigation about bouncing balls in their scheme of work they may choose a title such as "Does the surface affect bounciness?"
In this case the possible input variable might be: height of drop, surface, size of ball, material of ball, mass of ball.

The outcome variable might be: height of first bounce, number of bounces, length of time bounces continue.

The teacher may achieve differentiation between groups by managing the range of variables that each group is likely to handle.

A low achieving group might consider how just three or four surfaces affect the number of bounces of the ball.

An average group might investigate how the mass of the ball affects the height of the first bounce.

An able group might find out how the height of the drop affects the height of the first bounce and the time of bouncing.

Only a mature and confident group would investigate which has most effect on the bounce - the mass of the ball or the height from which it is dropped.

demand	input variable (independent)	example	outcome variable (dependent)	example
↓	categoric	*surface, material of ball*	discrete	*number of bounces*
	continuous	*mass of ball, height of drop*	continuous	*height of first bounce, time it bounces for*
	2 or more	*compare effect of changing mass and height*	derived	*velocity*

How Factors and Variables Affect Levels of Attainment in Sc1

The number and complexity of factors or variables used in practical work, in part determine the level of experimental and investigative science achieved. On their own the factors or variables do not define the level being achieved by the child.

Where teachers clearly understand the nature of factors or variables, they are able to encourage children to use the type of factors or variables most appropriate in any practical activity and hence promote children's progress in Sc1.

pupils accept factors or variables identified by the teacher	pupils recognise when a test is not fair when carried out by the teacher	pupils can carry out a fair test with help and recognise and explain why it is fair	pupils recognise the need for a fair test, can change one variable whilst controlling the others	pupils can identify the factors and variables where a few are involved and can focus on the key factors they need to consider
1	2	3	4	5

pupils can use knowledge and understanding to identify the key factors they need to consider in an increasingly complex range of investigations	pupils can identify the key factors from a number of factors, using knowledge and understanding	pupils can use knowledge and understanding to identify those factors they can control and those they cannot, in the increasing variety of experimental strategies they select to investigate their effects	pupils can select an appropriate strategy to investigate the effect of identified factors to be considered, recognising the wide range of strategies available, and choosing the most relevant, for the factors being investigated
6	7	8	exceptional performance

Chapter 5

Planning Experimental and Investigative Learning

page	48	Planning Experimental and Investigative Learning
	49	Planning for Effective Skills Acquisition
	49	Planning for Effective Illustrative Experiment
	50	Planning for Effective Investigation
	51	The Development of Investigative Learning
	52	The Context of Investigative Learning

Planning Experimental and Investigative Learning

During the development of schemes of work, teachers will allocate practical work to achieve specific purposes. There will be practical activities which are specifically planned to enable skill acquisition as well as experimental and investigative work. Illustrative experiments will be planned to ensure that recently taught knowledge and understanding is reinforced by active learning, and investigations will be planned so that children can develop further both skills and understanding in a new context involving their own ideas.

This chapter will outline how planning will ensure that the management of experimental and investigative learning takes place more effectively in the classroom:

- planning for effective skills acquisition

- planning for effective illustrative experiments

- planning for effective investigation

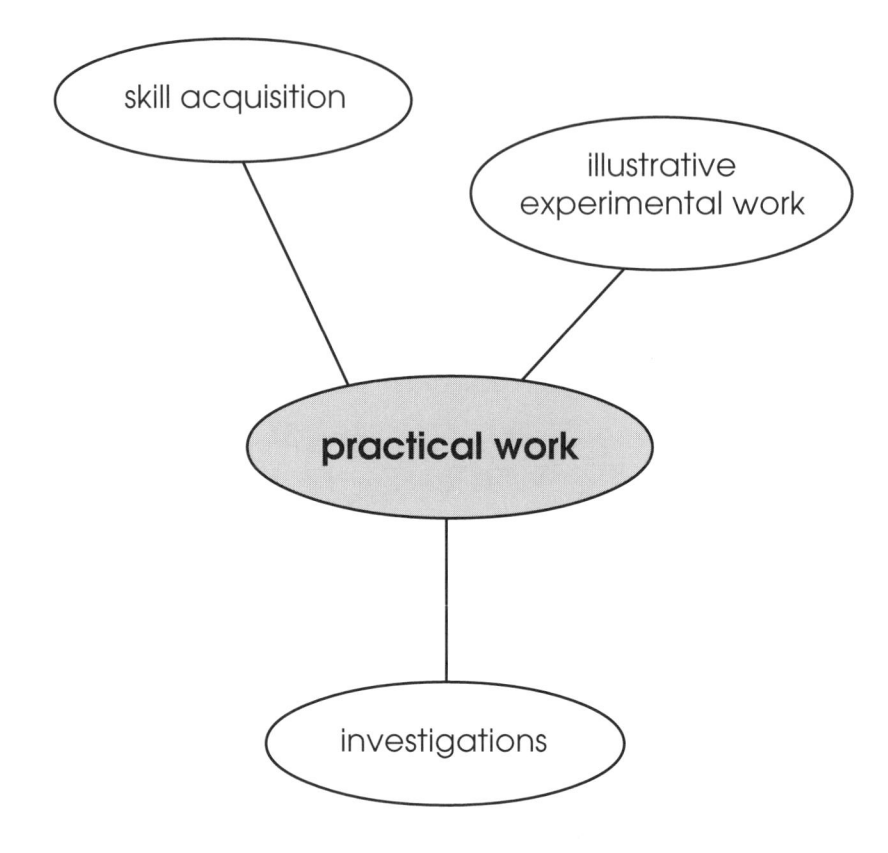

Planning for Effective Skills Acquisition

If the decision has been made that the skills to be acquired by the student are practical in nature, and can be consolidated by individual practice, then the learning objective for the lesson can be specified simply, eg:

1. To acquire and practise the skills of measuring temperature and volume.
2. The teacher can identify the apparatus necessary - in number and degree of accuracy appropriate to the skill being taught.
3. The skills of reading the measuring cylinder and the thermometer can be demonstrated, either in groups setting alternative work for the rest or to the whole class.

An experiment which uses the skills, and requires little else in terms of prior knowledge and understanding can be devised: eg What are the results when you mix different volumes of water at different temperatures?
Task sheets at different levels of difficulty could be set:

Experiment 1
Mix $50cm^3$ water at $20°C$ with $50cm^3$ at $40°C$
What is the resulting volume?
Is this what you would have expected?

Experiment 2
Mix $100cm^3$ water at $20°C$ with $50cm^3$ water at $40°C$
What is the resulting volume and temperature?
Was this surprising?
How could you make sure it is done more accurately?
Can you make a chart to collect your results?

Planning for Effective Illustrative Experiments

1. The teacher has decided to demonstrate the stretching of a spring. It will illustrate that the spring stretches by the same amount each time an equal load is hung on it.

2. The task can be set "What happens when loads are added onto a spring?" and identify the apparatus that will be needed by the class.

3. The concept of springs stretching can be discussed and the method of adding loads to the spring and taking measurements demonstrated. The directions, or instructions, can be written on a worksheet, eg:

Measure the length of the spring.
Add a 100g load onto the bottom of the spring; measure the amount the spring has stretched.
Record your results on a chart.
Add another 100g load to the first, and measure the stretch of the spring again.
Repeat this until you have 600g on the spring.
Do you see a pattern in your results?
Could you make a prediction about the extension of the spring if you add another 200g?

What load will produce a spring of .... cm overall?

Planning for Effective Investigation

Through investigation, children gain in their knowledge and understanding of science as well as developing their investigational skills. This may happen to a limited extent even without the advantage of good organisation by the teacher. Investigations must be carefully planned and prepared in order to capitalise on their full potential for learning. Although much of the decision-making within an investigation is made by the learners themselves, teachers do not lose their responsibilities for preparation, rather there is a change in emphasis of the role. The teacher has a different role when managing learning through investigations, although no less great than in other forms of practical learning.

Before children start investigations the teacher will need to:

- identify learning objectives - whole investigation detailed analysis of data etc

- decide how to initiate the investigation

- identify possible range of resources needed

- identify possible questions that can be used when teacher intervention is required

When a teacher is less familiar with children learning through investigations this planning process will be longer and more meticulous. With greater familiarity the planning becomes a quicker and more routine part of general preparation.

The teacher's role in investigative learning includes:

- identifying the learning objectives

- managing the class to achieve those learning objectives

- interacting with the children to help ensure learning

This is shown in more detail on the following diagram "The Development of Investigative Learning".

Plan -
- *learning objectives*
- *how to get started*
- *resources*
- *written support material*
- *questions you will ask*

The Development of Investigative Learning

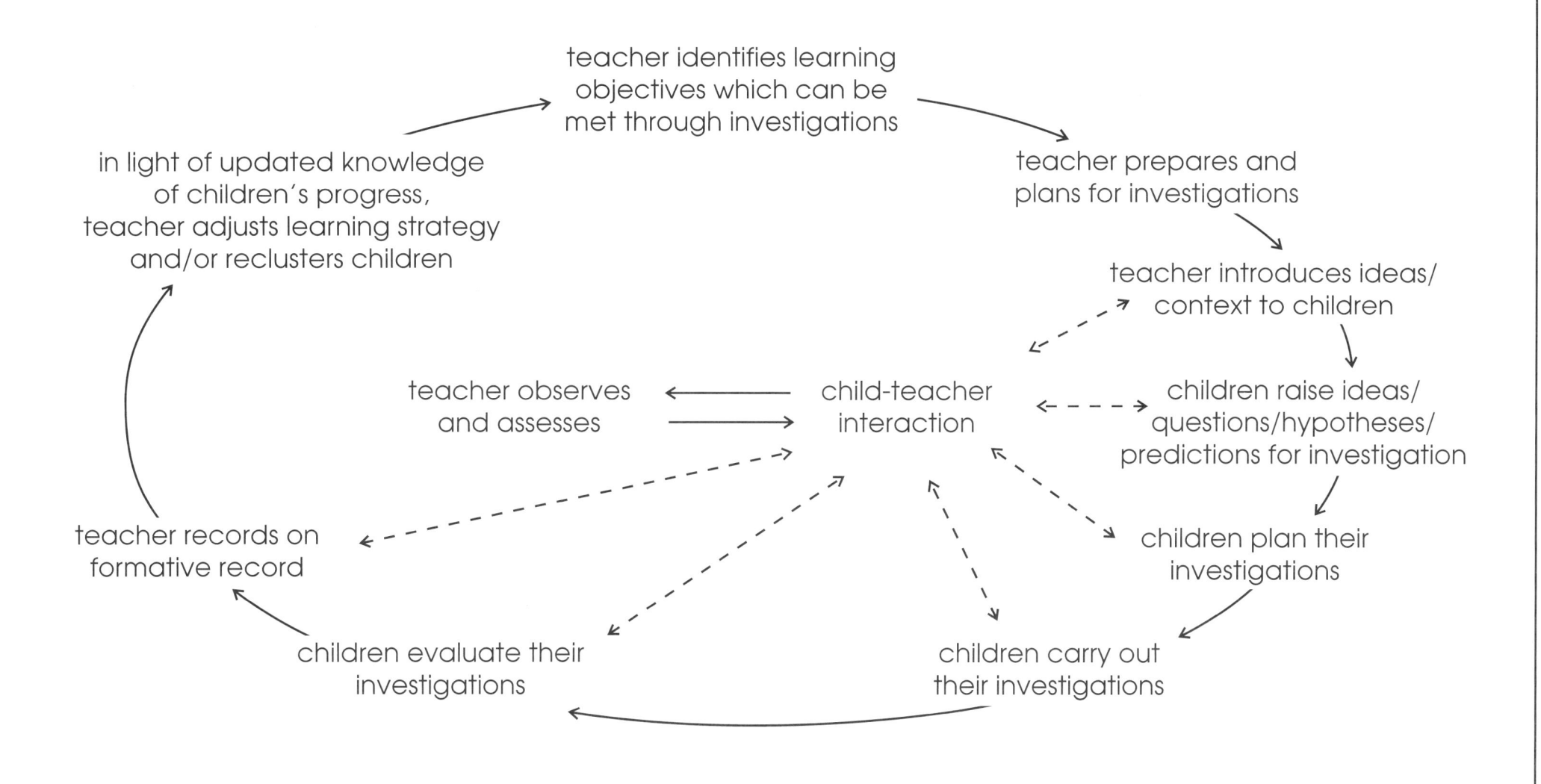

- teacher identifies learning objectives which can be met through investigations
- teacher prepares and plans for investigations
- teacher introduces ideas/context to children
- children raise ideas/questions/hypotheses/predictions for investigation
- children plan their investigations
- children carry out their investigations
- children evaluate their investigations
- child-teacher interaction
- teacher observes and assesses
- teacher records on formative record
- in light of updated knowledge of children's progress, teacher adjusts learning strategy and/or reclusters children

The Context of Investigative Learning

Investigations will usually be rooted in the Programmes of Study for science and teachers should use these to inform their planning. Some parts of the Programmes of Study will yield fewer opportunities for open investigations than others. Teachers often find Sc2, Variation and Classification, and Sc4 The Earth and Beyond, contain fewer opportunities for investigations. In these cases it may be necessary to use fewer investigations augmented by alternative methods of active learning rather than attempting to contrive inappropriate investigations.

It is necessary to make decisions about the degree of openness within the planned investigations. Under some circumstances the teacher will need to more tightly prescribe the bounds of the investigations. Such circumstances will include:

- teachers' and learners' experience of investigations
- resource limitations
- time scale
- the aspect of the Programme of Study being investigated
- safety implications

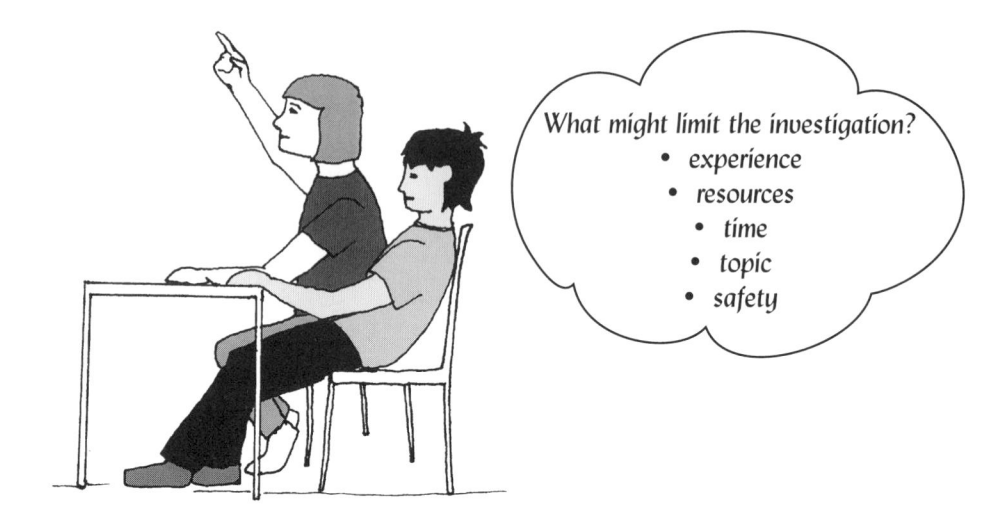

What might limit the investigation?
- *experience*
- *resources*
- *time*
- *topic*
- *safety*

In order to develop a scheme of work teachers will need to consider the progression of Sc1 skills and competencies and create a progressive list of learing objectives within each of the separate elements of Sc1.

To achieve these learning objectives teachers will offer opportunities for:

- skill organisation
- knowledge acquisition/reinforcement
- understanding and practising the scientific process

Chapter 6

Managing Experimental and Investigative Learning

page   54   Managing Experimental Practical Work
              56   Managing Investigative Learning
              57   Whole Class Brainstorming
              58   Supplementary Questioning
              59   Small Group Brainstorming
              60   Individual Hypothesising
              61   How Open is an Investigation?
              62   Starting Points for investigations
              63   Differentiation Through Starting Questions
              64   Managing Experimental and Investigative Learning

Managing Experimental Practical Work

Experimental work in science has the same philosophical base as investigative learning: the key objective is to promote pupils' scientific thinking. In experimental work this objective could be further refined as being the

A   development of understanding scientific methodology (ie how investigations progress)

B   refinement of particular investigative skills

C   deliberate development of scientific ideas or concepts, eg that forces can be balanced and that this explains floating

It is important for teachers always to be clear of the key objective since the strategy for managing the learning springs from this decision.

In experimental practical work, the frame of reference of the experiment and the course that it follows are usually made by the teacher. Many of the decisions that would be made by the pupils in investigative learning will instead be made by the teacher. The teacher may control almost all the elements of the experiment, leaving perhaps only one 'window' in which pupils' independent work is to happen.

A   Development of Scientific Methodology

The teacher may deliberately set out to lead pupils through an entire experiment, discussing all the decisions, and merely invite them to record the experiment.

B   Refinement of Particular Investigative Skills

The teacher may have, for example, the children's ability to set up and carry out a fair test as the objective. In this case, the teacher will lead the investigation through the stages leading up to this point, agreeing a common hypothesis and will then ask the pupils to list all the factors which might affect the outcome and to plan a method to carry out the experiment fairly. The pupils do this and record the outcomes using a ready-made format and the teacher will lead discussion on the interpretation of the results to achieve a shared conclusion.

C   Development of Scientific Ideas

A third possibility is that a scientific concept is the main objective. In this case the experiment is a familiar 'practical' which is set up to illustrate a scientific idea and has a known outcome. In this case the teacher makes all the decisions about resourcing and methodology but the pupils carry out the given procedure. The pupils are then invited to interpret the evidence they have gained. Thus they may be led to understand that granulated sugar dissolves more easily in hot water and with stirring and this provides the teacher with the opportunity to teach how dissolving happens and what factors are involved.

Trialing Experiments and Investigations

Experimental work differs from investigative work because many of the decisions that would be made by pupils (eg what to investigate, what hypothesis we have, how we will find out, what equipment will we need, how we will make it fair, how we will record, what interpretation we make of the evidence and what conclusion we might draw) - are now controlled by the teacher to achieve the chosen objective. The advantage of doing this is that it enables the teacher to:

- teach to specific needs, identified in ongoing assessment

- enable a quick route to scientific understanding which is still active learning and "hands on"

- assess specific capabilities in Sc1

- reinforce the holistic nature of the whole science process by leading pupils through it

Before launching into an experiment or investigation with a group of children it is necessary to trial the practical activity oneself. Without this brief trial it would be difficult to:

- evaluate the learning outcomes of the practical activity

- foresee the full resource implications of the practical activity

- judge the time management of the practical activity

- foresee any likely practical hitches which will require trouble shooting

- foresee any safety points which will need attention

- decide the likely limits to place on the scope of the practical activity

- prepare for when and where to intervene in the children's practical activity

- clarify the types of guidance the children will need and to prepare suitable enabling questions

Managing Investigative Learning

Generating Questions and Hypotheses for Investigations

Children can only progress in science investigations as a whole if they are able to develop abilities to raise ideas, questions, hypotheses and predictions. Without a sufficiently supportive climate in their classroom these abilities will not develop to best advantage.

Some teachers express reservations about how to help these abilities to develop. Some find it daunting that children's abilities to raise questions and hypotheses and predictions do not appear to be quickly developed or exhibited by all children in a group.

Four possible strategies for helping these abilities to develop are illustrated on the following pages. The strategies usually employ these aspects:

- providing an initial stimulus or common experience to focus children's attention

- the teacher posing an initial question to provoke further questions from the children

- discussion or other interaction between children or between child and teacher

- skillful intervention by the teacher to help children further refine their questions, hyphotheses, until in a form suitable for investigation

Without such strategies all children will rarely spontaneously ask questions for investigation or generate hypotheses; nor will they develop the ability to refine these into forms ready for investigation.

Skilled intervention will help refine questions into hypotheses which can be tested

I think the size of the grain affects how porous it is

The bigger the grains the better it is

Well, it will soak up more water - a bigger volume of water

Whole Class Brainstorm

Following a lesson in which young children have been observing woodlice

Are there any more questions about woodlice you want to add to our class list?

Can woodlice dig underground?

What do they like to eat?

Why do some woodlice roll up?

Which one of these questions do you want to investigate?

The whole class brainstorm questions on the same topic based on a common previous experience. Thus all children have an opportunity to contribute to the class list. The teacher helps the children to frame their questions. The class can then discuss the list, deciding which questions are most suitable for investigation and which would not be possible to investigate. Small groups of the children can select any questions from the list that they wish to investigate.

Supplementary Questioning

The teacher provides the initial stimulus in order to provoke supplementary questions from the children.
In this case at the start of a topic on dissolving

- Now that you've all got one of the sweets in your mouth-
- What can you tell me about the taste?
- I think it's prickly and fizzy
- What do you think it's doing?
- It feels funny on my tongue
- Is it bubbling in my mouth?
- What exactly do you mean by "funny"?
- Is it going colder in my mouth?

The teacher provides the initial stimulus and poses the initial question "What can you tell me about the taste?" focused on the topic being studied.

Children raise other points and supplementary questions which the teacher guides towards an idea or question that can be investigated.

Small Group Brainstorming

The whole class have started a study of friction by observing the different grip of various shoes on a sloping wooden plank. Later the class will work in small groups

You've all seen how the different shoes slide down the slope

I want each group to think of the things which might affect how the shoe slides

Is it the steepness that causes it?

I think it might be the tread that's more important

Doesn't the smoothness of the plank affect it?

I think the stuff the sole is made from is most important

The teacher has led the whole class into the investigations through the initial demonstration of shoes slipping down a slope. The teacher prompts questions by asking "What might affect.....?" Each small group can brainstorm their ideas of the factors involved and then select which factor(s) they will investigate. Further questions to each group by the teacher might help them to reformulate their ideas into a form which can be investigated.

Individual Hypothesising

On a few occasions an individual learner may suggest their own hypothesis or question.
Towards the end of a topic on weathering and erosion ....

What aspect of sandstone weathering are you going to investigate?

What sort of affect do you mean?

What exactly do you mean by "better"?

I think the size of the grain affects how porous it is

The bigger the grains the better it is

Well, it will soak up more water - a bigger volume of water

The individual learner has decided which aspect of the work to investigate - based on earlier learning. Careful questioning by the teacher helps the hypothesis to be formulated in a way suitable for investigation.

How Open is an Investigation?

Most scientific investigations are relatively open in that the outcome, or the route to that outcome, has not been wholly pre-determined by the teacher. Whilst managing the learning of the class the teacher will make decisions about how open or closed an investigation needs to be for a particular group or individual child.

The openness of an investigation can be largely governed by the degree to which the input (independent) and outcome (dependent) variables are defined in the starting question of an investigation.

An investigation that starts from a question provided by the teacher, "What effect does the temperature of the water have on the time it takes sugar to dissolve?", has both the input and outcome variables pre-defined. This largely pre-determines the outcome achieved by the children and to a considerable extent the route they will take. This closed investigation will make less demands in many ways and will considerably limit the potential level of attainment of the children.

In contrast, a much more open investigation would result from the starting question, "What affects how fizzers dissolve?". The children will have to define their own input variable (eg temperature) and the outcome variables (eg time). This may make greater demands on the children and on the teacher managing the investigation, but it offers the children much more opportunity for achievement in Sc1. It allows children of widely differing abilities the opportunity to reach an appropriate level of attainment.

Important judgements have to be made about the learning needs of their children based on factors such as:

- maturity and ability
- experience of and confidence in investigative work
- their position within the topic or subject matter being studied
- the learning objectives decided by the teacher

In general, the use of more open investigations allows for greater differentiation in achievement in Sc1.

Starting points can be tailored to need by controlling the degree of openness.

Starting Points for Investigations

Many teachers use trigger questions such as "How do shadows change during the day?" as starting points for investigations.

These trigger questions are intended, as the name implies, as points from which the teacher can start discussion with the whole class, groups or individuals, or from where children can discuss amongst themselves the scope and exact nature of their own investigation. Once again it is important that the teacher uses their professional skill to ensure each group or individual is guided into an investigation of appropriate complexity.

The starting points that follow vary in their degree of openness and therefore offer a range of opportunities for adaption into individual investigations. This is illustrated through four examples:

- "What things will a magnet pick up?" has most of the factors predetermined and therefore offers young children considerable guidance as a starting point

- "What is the effect of exercise on heart rate?" provides the children with a defined outcome (dependent) variable but requires the children to decide the factors that they will investigate and allows them to predict the likely effects

- "What conditions make large crystals grow best?" requires a decision about what is meant by "best" in this question. Therefore none of the variables are defined and it provides opportunity for investigations at a variety of levels

- "Investigate the transfer of energy in the food chain of a ladybird" provides very little guidance and requires considerable discussion and decisions by more mature children possibly with their teacher in order to make a more precise definition of the investigation to be undertaken

Such trigger questions are suitable for use in more than one key stage. Because of the overlap between key stages a question such as "What factors affect the shadow formed?" might be used at key stages 2, 3 or 4. Such starting points offer scope for children and teachers to refine and differentiate them to appropriate degrees of complexity.

Differentiation Through Starting Questions

A teacher within key stage 2 whose class is studying dissolving may select "What type of sugar dissolves fastest?" as a possible starting point. This question is not given directly to all children in the class to investigate, rather it is used as the stimulus for a class brainstorm. Differentiation within the class is achieved through a variety of questions and ideas being raised.

A small group that requires a lot of support might be guided to investigate the question "Which type of sugar is the first to dissolve?" In this question two simple categoric variables are defined for the group. Children already capable of investigating at a higher level could tackle a much more open question such as, "What makes sugar dissolve best?". For this question the children have to decide what is meant by best and to select a number of variables to investigate (volume, temperature, stirring, etc).

Differentiation across key stages can also be achieved. The same starting point could be used by a teacher at key stage 3 or 4 whose class is studying solubility. The teacher could modify it and present the class with the more open question "What affects solubility?". This would allow children to investigate the effect of a variety of variables (solvent, solute, temperature, etc) to increasing levels of sophistication.

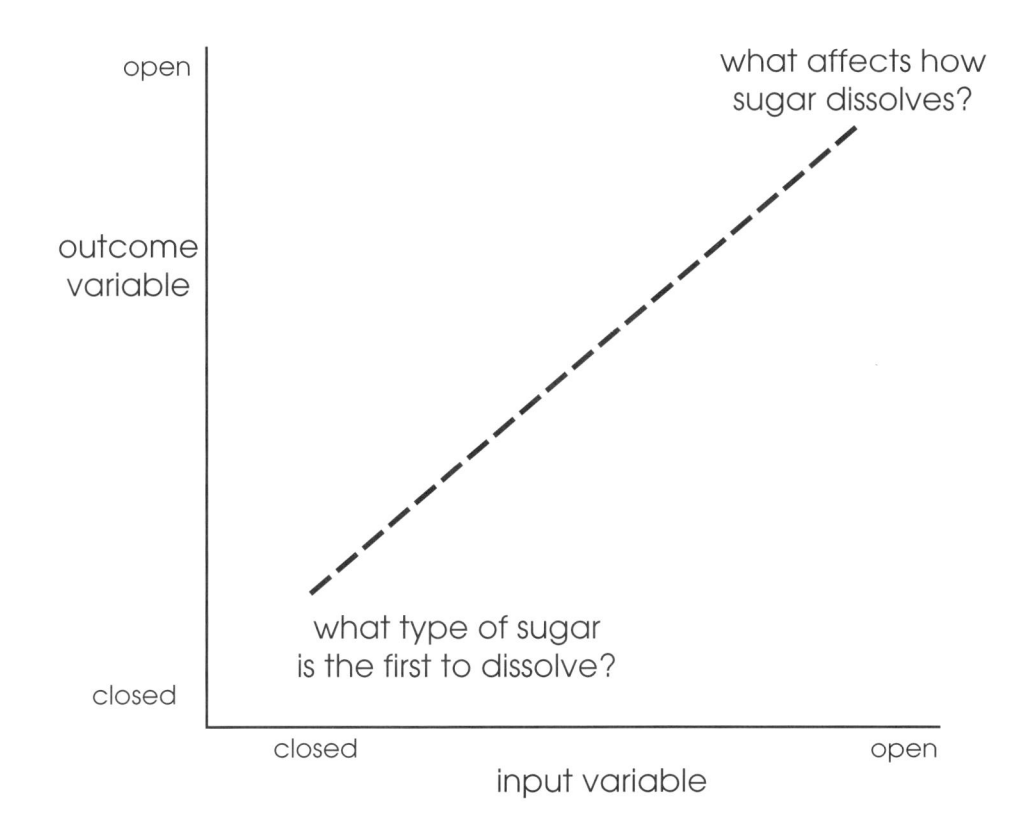

Careful choice of starting questions can provide a range of opportunities from closed investigations, where the variables are pre-determined, to open investigations where children have to make all the decisions about the variables.

Managing Experimental and Investigative Learning

This chapter outlined the management of experimental work and the management of investigative learning. In chapter 1 (page 2) these two types of learning were described as the extremes of the practical science continuum. They should not be thought of as two distinct isolated approaches to practical science.

Both experimental and investigative learning enables children to think scientifically.

Practical work in science can be characterised as experiment or investigation

Experimental practical work can be managed to achieve:
- *improved scientific methodology*
- *improved investigative skills*
- *increased scientific understanding*

Investigations often, but not always, start from pupils' own ideas or hypotheses

Ways of promoting hypotheses include:
- *whole class brainstorm*
- *supplementary questioning*
- *small group brainstorm*
- *individual hypothesising*

By controlling the openness of an investigation starting question you can manage demand and achieve differentiation

Chapter 7

Organising Classrooms and Resources

page 66 Organising Classrooms and Resources
      68 Planning for safety in Experimental and Investigative Work
      70 Strategies for Developing an Understanding About Safety

Organising Classrooms and Resources

In order for progress to be made in investigational skills the classroom or laboratory needs to provide opportunities for independent work and to enable children to make decisions and act upon them. There are two main aspects of organisation that may aid this independent learning:

- organisation of resources
- classroom organisation

Organisation of Resources

Resources need to be accessible for children to select and use. Within Sc1 children are explicitly required to select measuring instruments at level 4 and above and consequently require access to a range of measuring instruments from which to choose. Children's performance in designing investigations is almost always improved when they have access to equipment before they begin to plan, compared to occasions when planning is essentially a paper and pencil activity. Lack of access to equipment is likely to hinder achievement in scientific investigation.

Every primary classroom should have a minimum of science equipment in order to capitalise on everyday opportunities for science. Items such as hand lenses, magnets, simple circuit kit, mirrors, torches, glue and scissors and measuring equipment will need to be in all classrooms on a permanent basis.

In the secondary school laboratories will need a wider range of equipment, including basic glassware, heating apparatus, retort stands etc. In both cases these will need to be stored in an accessible place which is clearly marked, ideally with both the name and an outline drawing, and numbered or identified to facilitate easy return and checking.

Other resources which will be drawn from a central store for practical work should also be clearly marked and the container given a prominent position, so that children are both provided with a good visual stimulus of possible resources and are less restricted in their selection of equipment.

The Programmes of Study refer to the need for children to use information technology in the course of practical work. This can involve the use of sensors for data capture, information storage, transfer and retrieval, use of spreadsheets and databases, as well as for presentation of their work. Computers and other information technology with their associated software will need to be made as accessible as possible to the children.

Classroom Organisation

In order to best develop the practical and thinking skills during practical activities the class will need to be organised to give children easy access to resources and the teacher access to the children.

The management of this learning will require careful planning in order that:

- all children have the opportunity to take part in practical work on a regular basis

- those children engaged in practical activities will probably need to have more of the teacher's attention. This might result in other children being engaged in less supervised work which will need to be purposeful rather than merely palliative

- essential resources are available and accessible to the children

- the work offered to the children is part of a continuum of increasingly open-ended and independent whole investigations. Children are gradually able to make more and more decisions about how and when they investigate, what and how they measure and record, and what and how they communicate

- the type and membership of groups can be decided to maximise learning opportunities. Teachers will choose appropriate groupings from friendship, mixed ability, single sex, pairs, larger groups, etc

- an estimate of time needed for the practical activity can be made, and consideration given to extension or reinforcement activities for children who complete their practical activities early

Management of
- *grouping*
- *children's activity*
- *resources*
- *time*

Planning for Safety in Experimental and Investigative work

The National Curriculum in England and Wales (1995) places a requirement on children to recognise hazards and consider risks, and particularly for older children to assess risks and take action to control them. Teachers may mistakenly interpret this as children being responsible for risk assessment. Health and safety legislation places a requirement on the employer to undertake risk assessment and therefore the requirements outlined in the National Curriculum relate to the part children will play in **risk analysis**.

Sc1 will provide the main vehicle through which risk analysis will occur. It places a greater emphasis on children being helped to:

- understand some of the hazards associated with the materials and operations they use
- consider the risks of their planned activities
- find out about the degree of risk (risk analysis)
- ask advice of teachers and other adults
- consider ways of reducing risks
- think carefully about their own and other people's safety

Children's involvement in these six points is in itself a fruitful learning activity and a valuable part of their scientific education which will be helpful in their future careers and in adult life. Children's ability to appreciate and manage their safety is a progressive development, ranging, for example from:

- asking whether they are allowed to use scissors (at key stage 1)
- consulting a Hazcard about the risk of using 4M hydrochloric acid in a rate of reaction investigation, asking their teacher's permission and requesting plastic gloves from the technician (at key stage 4).

Children should be involved in developing their own understanding of risk and safety throughout their education. Experimental and investigative work offers an excellent context in which children can progressively develop their understanding of risk and abilities to assess and manage risks.

This means a changed role for the classroom teacher in managing safety, particularly at key stages 3 and 4. It is particularly important that teachers trial investigations before children start them so that they are more aware of the risks which are likely to occur.

Teachers must make judgements about whether the risks involved in the investigation can be limited and managed successfully, either by the children or by themselves. If the investigation is judged to involve too great a risk then it cannot proceed in the anticipated manner. The most extreme remedy will be to substitute non-practical work, more directed experimental work or a demonstration for the proposed investigation.

Alternative strategies include:
- introduce greater safeguards into the investigation
- curtail the investigation to avoid the main risk
- introduce some second-hand data into the investigation that cirumvent the need for the higher risk operation
- reduce the number of children carrying out the investigation, giving non-practical tasks to others in the class
- ensuring that the parts of the investigation with the greatest risk are only carried out under adult supervision

Some teachers may find it helpful to classify children's activities as red, amber and green as a way of judging and managing practical activities.

red activities   - greater risk; a lot of direct supervision required
amber activities   - medium risk; some direct supervision required
green activities   - low risk; little direct supervision required

This classification can then be used in organising classroom activity.

Only one red activity should operate at any one time:

perhaps • a demonstration by the teacher
or   • a demonstration by a closely supervised small group, watched by others
or   • one group working and closely supervised by the teacher whilst the rest of the class are all involved in green or non-practical activities

Two or three groups may be carrying out amber activities, positioned by the teacher so that they are most conveniently supervised. Other children would be engaged in green activities.

Any number of green activities might be operating at any time.

An essential part of planning for safety is to ensure that the school has:

- a policy for safety in science education
- necessary safety information about investigations documented within the schemes of work
- essential safety information such as "Be Safe!" or Hazcards or "Safeguards In The School Laboratory" readily available for reference by teachers and support staff
- strategies for systematically developing children's understanding of safety

Strategies for Developing an Understanding About Safety

Such strategies for developing understanding of safety will vary with the age and experience of the children but may include:

- rules for classroom behaviour
- laboratory safety rules
- safety pointers on children's investigation planning sheet
- a safety planning/reminder sheet for investigations
- access for children to standard safety information (posters, "Be Safe!", cards, etc)
- an expectation that pupils will require their plan for the investigation to be referred to their teacher
- a rule that children do not start an investigation unless sanctioned by a teacher/adult
- access to safety equipment such as steel safety rules, safety spectacles, etc.

A Useful Safety Reference List

Primary:

Be Safe! - 2nd edition (ASE) 1990

Health and Safety Activities Book (NIAS) 1995

Secondary:

Safety in Science Education (DfEE, HMSO) 1996

Safeguards in the School Laboratory - 10th edition (ASE) 1996

Laboratory Handbook (CLEAPSS) 1989 - with 1991, 1992, 1994 and 1995 additions

Hazcards (CLEAPSS) 1995

Microbiology: an HMI Guide for Schools and Further Education (HMSO) 1990

Topics in Safety - 2nd edition (ASE) 1988
(3rd edition in preparation 1997)

Safety Reprints (ASE) 1996

Hazardous Chemicals Manual (SSERC)
(new edition in preparation 1996)

Chapter 8

Strategies for Teacher Intervention During Experimental and Investigative Science Activities

page 72 Appropriate Use of Language
73 Written and Verbal Intervention
74 Planning Sheets
75 Experimental and Investigation Planning Sheet
79 Advanced Experimental and Investigation Planning Sheet
83 Oral Reporting of Experiments and Investigations
83 Asking Enabling Questions
85 Enabling Question Planner

Appropriate Use of Language

The skilled use of language is essential for effective learning in most situations.

This is equally true for learning through investigations and therefore an important part of managing investigative learning is to plan aspects of the language to be used. This has several important purposes:

- helping to maintain clear communication between teacher and learner

- highlighting vocabulary which may need to be introduced, explained or extended

- indicating the match or mismatch between language and concept development

- enabling access to appropriate levels of attainment by all children

Appropriate use of language can enable access to higher levels of attainment by deliberately engineering opportunities and cues for learners to demonstrate their understanding and achievement of statements of attainment. Lack of planning in use of language by teachers may close doors upon potential opportunities for learners to demonstrate their achievement of these higher levels.

Planning the language to be used during an investigation is therefore important whether it be in preparing written materials (planning sheets, information cards, prompt sheets etc), preparing enabling questions (see later in this chapter) or simply talking to children to help them during investigations.

Carefully planned language helps children to
- *progress*
- *demonstrate their achievement*

Written and Verbal Intervention

Many teachers find a planning sheet or a structured set of subheadings helpful in guiding children's progress, which is an example of written intervention in children's learning. At other times a well judged question asked of the child by the teacher may be the best way of allowing the child to advance their experiment or investigation and to demonstrate their ability.

Both written and verbal intervention by the teacher have key roles in advancing children's learning and helping to assess their achievement. The potential advantages and disadvantages of each type of intervention are summarised below.

	potential advantages	potential disadvantages
verbal intervention	<ul><li>immediate response and feedback possible</li><li>modification or further explanation easily possible</li><li>more easily targeted to a particular child, experiment, investigation or detail</li><li>more personal</li></ul>	<ul><li>fewer children reached</li><li>evidence of attainment is ephemeral</li><li>more likely to be forgotten or delayed during lesson</li></ul>
written intervention	<ul><li>more children reached</li><li>greater consistency possible</li><li>more likely to produce written evidence of attainment</li></ul>	<ul><li>feedback delayed (perhaps next day or next week)</li><li>less personal and the "colder" information is less likely to be acted upon</li><li>children with reading difficulties are disadvantaged</li><li>less targeted, blanket coverage</li><li>less easily modified or explained</li></ul>

Planning Sheets for Experimental and Investigative Work

Planning sheets are increasingly used with children especially at key stages 3 and 4, as an aid to both helping children plan (and later to record) and managing the work of their class. Such planning sheets help children of sufficient maturity to structure their practical work and to record evidence. Use of the sheets can help teachers to identify:

- apparatus likely to be needed
- suggested apparatus that is likely to be inappropriate
- safety considerations
- children who are likely to make little progress without further guidance
- possible regrouping of children for more effective learning
- evidence of achievement in Sc1, particularly in planning, and in manipulation of variables

Planning sheets can also help children make statements and answers to questions which they would seldom suggest unprompted, such as giving a scientific reason for their hypothesis.

However, there can be a temptation at key stages 3 and 4 for planning sheets to become a formal exercise conducted only for assessment purposes. In these situations children tend to work individually, under test conditions with no use of apparatus until the following lesson. This tends to make investigations take a long time and produce large amounts of written work, much of it unnecessary.

The planning sheet that follows is intended for use by children at the top of key stage 2 or at key stages 3 or 4, as part of the normal lesson routine. Where appropriate, children should have equipment available to help in their planning. It is not intended to be used "cold", as an assessment tool, although it will aid children in recording some evidence of achievement and can provide an opportunity for teacher annotation to record ephemeral evidence.

The sheet might be adapted to make it more appropriate to particular classes by, for example, using more space for answers, ruled lines for writing etc.

The completed example of a planning sheet indicates how the teacher's marking of the sheet has been used to guide the child's learning through formative assessment and how it can be used by the teacher to record the child's spoken comment, as ephemeral evidence of achievement.

Children who are confident in investigation and are working at level 6 or above, and with sound literary skills, are likely to need a more specialised sheet. This will have more space for recording results, provision for follow-on sheets, and will include greater guidance for achievement in the higher levels. An example is provided on pages 77 to 81.

The documents included in Chapter 10, intended to help children recognise and advance their own learning, may prove helpful.

Experiment and Investigation Planning Sheet

Name:

Class:

What I want to find out…

What I think will happen and why…

My scientific reason for thinking this…

How I will do the experiment…

How I will make it safe…

To make sure the experiment is fair, these things must not change…

Equipment I will need to use…

My results...

What my results mean...

How my results compare to what I thought would happen...

I could improve what I did by...

Experiment and Investigation Planning Sheet

Name: Alexander Borton
Others in my group: Chris, Sam, Jo.
Class: 7DW

What I want to find out...

Which sort of ball bounces best?

What I think will happen and why...

I think the tennis ball will win because I know tennis balls bounce high.

My scientific reason for thinking this...

It's hard and it's got air in

(circled note: air squeezed (ie compressed) and pushes on the floor as the ball bounces)

How I will do the experiment...

We're going to push each ball off the table, then Chris will measure how high it bounces. We will do each ball twice. We've got a tennis ball, a sponge ball, an airflow ball, a super ball, a marble and a metal ball.

How I will make it safe...

We'll catch them before they roll away — because they might make people fall over.

To make sure the experiment is fair, these things must not change...

The height we drop them from. The way we push them off.
Who does the pushing. What they land on.

Equipment I will need to use...

The balls I've already told you about.
A table
A ruler to push the balls off
A big ruler to measure how high they go.

My results...

	1st try	2nd try
Tennis	30 cm	32 cm ✱
Sponge	8 cm	
Air flo	26 cm	9 cm ✱
Super ball	56 cm	
Marble	25 cm	
Metal ball	12 cm	

✱ Alex, can you explain why these two are different?

How my results compare to what I thought would happen...

What my results mean...

I could improve what I did by...

I don't think we did anything wrong.
① Please finish your second go - will you need more?
② Does it matter what they bounce on?
③ Have you changed your mind about what makes a ball a good bouncer?

Advanced Investigation Planning Sheet

Name:

Class:

The hypothesis you are testing:

The scientific knowledge or theory you are using:

Any outcomes or measurements you predict:

Brief outline of how you will carry out the investigation:

This page is copyright waived

All the factors that could affect your investigation:

Variables you decide to change (input variables):

The variable that will change as a result (outcome variable):

	1st input variable changed	2nd input variable changed
input variable that you will change		
controlled variables that you will keep the same whilst changing one input variable; other factors you will need to take account of		
outcome variable that you will measure		

The range of measurements taken, and why:

How you arranged to get sufficiently accurate and reliable results:

Information gathered from other people, books and other sources

Your results:

What your results mean:

Any other meanings your results could have:

This page is copyright waived

Patterns you find in your results:	Why any results didn't fit the pattern:	How accurate and reliable your results are:	How well your results support your original hypothesis:	Any changes you made to your hypothesis:	Any follow up that is needed:	Changes that could be made to your investigation:

Oral Reporting of Experiments and Investigations

Children in key stage 1 and early key stage 2, and many of those with learning difficulties, will tend to report their investigations orally. Children should be encouraged to report in the way that is most appropriate for both their ability and the demands of the investigation.

Thus year 4 children who have investigated, "What makes a paper towel a good mopper-upper?", but whose writing skills are not well developed, might be asked to report orally. On the other hand some year 2 children investigating, "Which car rolls furthest down the hill?", but who have good writing skills, might be asked to add some simple sentences to their pictures and to write down their key measurements.

Enabling questions which are intended to advance children's learning can also be modified as prompts to guide children's oral and written reporting. See pages 86 - 90.

Asking Enabling Questions

While children are carrying out experimental and investigative work, teachers will need to ask them questions in order to:

- promote an investigative attitude in children (providing only answers can hinder the development of this attitude)

- encourage and support their learning and to help initiate their investigations

- encourage and assist children with procedural difficulties, such as assembly of equipment or measuring

- provide an opportunity for access to the next level of attainment

If answers are supplied to children at inappropriate points in practical work or if teachers ask questions that close down options, achievement at a higher level may be prevented. Enabling questions are of critical importance: questions that enable children to make progress.

Therefore careful consideration must be given to the questions that will be asked during the investigation. Initially this will mean planning the questions before the lesson.

An enabling questions planner follows, with four examples of how it might be used, at each of the key stages.

An enabling questions planner serves several purposes:

- it leads stage by stage through the parts of a whole investigation and enables a cumulative grasp of the whole Sc1 process

- it achieves the key learning objectives of Sc1 because in order to make a child hypothesise, plan, measure... we ask a question that necessitates that outcome. Thus it enables refinement of each of these skills. The initial question will often need to be followed up by more probing or more supportive questioning

- Because the teaching style involved uses open questions pupils have to think and respond. This gives excellent evidence of pupils' levels of achievement and is therefore an invaluable assessment

Enabling questions help **both** to teach
                                    and to assess

What do you think will happen?

I think the bigger sweet will take longer to dissolve

Enabling Questions Planner

Learning Objectives	Starting Point:	Sc1 (PoS) References
considering factors and fair testing		
resourcing		
predicting		
using equipment		
observing and measuring		
organising evidence		
analysing and explaining		
evaluating		

How to Use the Enabling Questions Planner

Enabling Questions Planner (KS2)

Learning Objectives	Starting Point: What Makes a Ball a Good Bouncer?	Sc1 (PoS) References
considering factors and fair testing	How will you find out if your idea is true? Tell me exactly or write down how you might find out?	1a
resourcing	How will you make sure that your investigation is a fair test?	1d
predicting	What do you think will happen when you drop the ball?	
using equipment	What are you going to need for your investigation?	1e
observing and measuring	Will you need to measure anything? What?	1e, 2a
organising evidence	What is the best way of remembering what happens? How will you know what happened today if I ask you next week?	3a
analysing and explaining	What do the results mean? What does this tell you about the way these balls bounce? What's the best way of telling the rest of the class about what you've found out?	3b - 3c 3a, 3e
evaluating	How good was your test, could you improve on it?	2c, 3d

— the main subject or starting point of the investigation

— questions that the teacher plans to ask in order to advance children's learning or reveal achievement of a learning objective

— identifying questions that specifically target single (or small ranges of) bullet points in the Programme of Study

— the key elements of the scientific process which represent the important learning objectives of experimental and investigative science

Enabling Questions Planner KS1

Learning Objectives	Starting Point: What Makes Refreshers Disappear?	Sc1 (PoS) References
considering factors and fair testing	How much water will we need? Should they all have the same? What about stirring?	1c
resourcing	What things will we need to use?	2a - 2c
predicting	What makes refreshers disappear in your mouth?	1a
using equipment	What will we use to measure how long it is?	2a - 2c
observing and measuring	How can you tell how quickly each one disappears?	2b
organising evidence	How will we remember which one was best? At the end of the afternoon tell everyone what you did.	3a - 3b 3a, 3f
analysing and explaining	Which one was quickest? What do you think makes refreshers disappear, now? Is it what you thought at first?	3c - 3d 3e
evaluating	Was this a good test? Could we have made it better?	3e

Enabling Questions Planner (KS2)

Learning Objectives	Starting Point: What Makes a Ball a Good Bouncer?	Sc1 (PoS) References
considering factors and fair testing	How will you find out if your idea is true? Tell me exactly or write down how you might find out?	1a
resourcing	How will you make sure that your investigation is a fair test?	1d
predicting	What do you think will happen when you drop the ball?	
using equipment	What are you going to need for your investigation?	1e
observing and measuring	Will you need to measure anything? What?	1e, 2a
organising evidence	What is the best way of remembering what happens? How will you know what happened today if I ask you next week?	3a
analysing and explaining	What do the results mean? What does this tell you about the way these balls bounce? What's the best way of telling the rest of the class about what you've found out?	3b - 3c 3a, 3e
evaluating	How good was your test, could you improve on it?	2c, 3d

Enabling Questions Planner (KS3)

Learning Objectives	Starting Point: What Affects How Quickly Refreshers Dissolve?	Sc1 (PoS) References
considering factors and fair testing	What are the main stages in your investigation? In what order will you do them? If you are changing the temperature, what will you have to keep the same?	1b, 1f 1e
resourcing	How can you change what happens in your mouth into laboratory tests?	1a
predicting	What makes refreshers dissolve quickly in your mouth? How many factors can you think of? Which do you think will have the most effect? Why?	1c - 1d
using equipment	You can get hot water from the urn - is there anything else on the bench or in the trays that you will need? Do you need to ask the technician for any other equipment?	1h, 2a
observing and measuring	How can you decide when it has finished dissolving? What is the hottest/coldest temperature you think you will need to test it at? Are your measurements as accurate as you can make them? Are your results valid?	2b - 2d
organising evidence	Can you put your results in a table? What headings will you use? What about the units? Do your results go best in a table/chart/graph?	2e 3a - 3c
analysing and explaining	What do your results mean? Can you analyse your results? Was your prediction right? Are your results reliable? Is there a mathematical pattern in your results? Which has the most effect on dissolving the refresher? Which has the least? How do you know? What is the best way to tell others what you did and what you found out?	3d - 3f 3e - 3f 3h
evaluating	What do your results mean? Is that always true? What else could your results mean? How can you tell that is what your results really mean?	4a 4b 4c

Enabling Questions Planner (KS4)

Learning Objectives	Starting Point: Potential & Kinetic Energy Conversions Involved in the Bouncing of the Ball	Sc1 (PoS) References
considering factors and fair testing	What are the main stages of your investigation? In what order will you do things? How many variables are there that you can test the effects of? What variables will you need to control/keep constant?	1a 1d 1e
resourcing	Are there any preliminary tests you need to carry out before starting the main investigation?	1b
predicting	What do you think might affect the way a ball bounces? What factor do you think has the biggest effect?	1c 1d
using equipment	What apparatus and materials will you need? What measuring instruments will be best for your investigation?	1h 2a, 2f
observing and measuring	How will you ensure your measurements are correct enough for the results you expect? What degree of accuracy do you think you can get? Are your results valid?	2a, 2c 2b
organising evidence	What is the best way to record your results? Could they be recorded in other ways - electronically or datalogged?	2f 3a
analysing and explaining	What do your results really mean? Is there another meaning these results could have? Is there a (mathematical) pattern in your results? Are your results reliable? What conclusions can you draw from your results? Are they what you expected? How do your results support your ideas/hypothesis/prediction? What is the most appropriate way of telling others about your investigation and results?	4a 3c 3a - 3b, 4b 4a 3a - 3e, 3h
evaluating	What was the point of your investigation? If someone else repeated the investigation how similar would their results be? Why? How sure are you about your results/conclusion? Now tell me just how good the theory/idea you were testing really was.	3g 4c - 4e 3f 3h

Chapter 9

How Can We Recognise Attainment in Sc1?

page	92	How Can We Recognise Attainment in Sc1?
	94	Indicators of Levelness - Bouncing Ball Activity
	98	Indicators of Levelness - Solubility Activity
	102	Some Possible Milestones - Assessing Sc1
	104	Summative Assessment

How Can We Recognise Attainment in Sc1?

This chapter is intended to help teachers understand the progression within Sc1 and to gain a feel for what each level means. It is not about the mechanism of making end of key stage assessments in Sc1, but it does relate to formative assessment judgements made in the classroom by teachers.

A short section such as this cannot define the exact meaning of Sc1 at all levels; for such definitions reference would need to be made to SCAA documents such as, "Children's Work Assessed, KS1", "Pupils' Work Assessed KS3", teacher consistency booklets and examination group guidance. However, this chapter is a user-friendly overview of the way in which the levels in Sc1 develop. It is intended to help teachers in their routine formative assessment by recognising attainment of individual children and moving them on to the next stage of their learning.

Indicators of Levelness

The next eight pages amplify the increasing level of difficulty for two areas of possible practical activity:

- bouncing balls and their energy
- dissolving

In each case the practical activity is illustrated to give an indication of the degree of complexity involved through each of the levels, showing what a child might be saying, writing or thinking. These pictures cannot attempt to give comprehensive coverage of all the level descriptions in an experiment or investigation. The illustrations are followed by a more comprehensive exemplification of what a child might say or write which indicates their likely level in each aspect of an experiment or investigation.

These bubbles give an indication of levelness

They are formative assessment indicators

Indicators of Levelness - Exemplified

The sequence of illustrations below provides an indication of levelness for two practical activities exemplified in this chapter

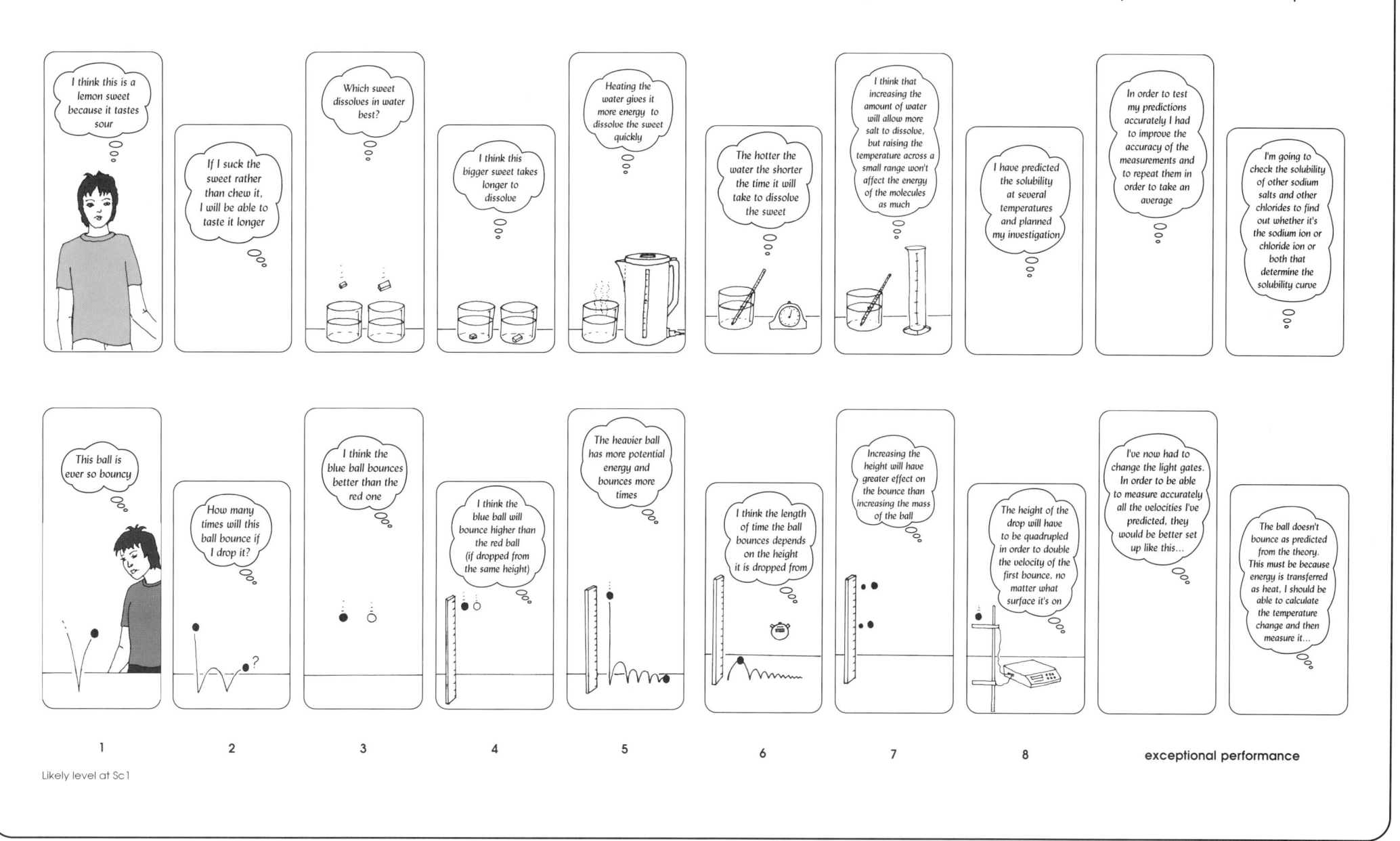

Row 1 (Sweets/Dissolving):

1. I think this is a lemon sweet because it tastes sour
2. If I suck the sweet rather than chew it, I will be able to taste it longer
3. Which sweet dissolves in water best?
4. I think this bigger sweet takes longer to dissolve
5. Heating the water gives it more energy to dissolve the sweet quickly
6. The hotter the water the shorter the time it will take to dissolve the sweet
7. I think that increasing the amount of water will allow more salt to dissolve, but raising the temperature across a small range won't affect the energy of the molecules as much
8. I have predicted the solubility at several temperatures and planned my investigation
9. In order to test my predictions accurately I had to improve the accuracy of the measurements and to repeat them in order to take an average
10. I'm going to check the solubility of other sodium salts and other chlorides to find out whether it's the sodium ion or chloride ion or both that determine the solubility curve

Row 2 (Bouncing balls):

1. This ball is ever so bouncy
2. How many times will this ball bounce if I drop it?
3. I think the blue ball bounces better than the red one
4. I think the blue ball will bounce higher than the red ball (if dropped from the same height)
5. The heavier ball has more potential energy and bounces more times
6. I think the length of time the ball bounces depends on the height it is dropped from
7. Increasing the height will have greater effect on the bounce than increasing the mass of the ball
8. The height of the drop will have to be quadrupled in order to double the velocity of the first bounce, no matter what surface it's on
9. I've now had to change the light gates. In order to be able to measure accurately all the velocities I've predicted, they would be better set up like this...
10. The ball doesn't bounce as predicted from the theory. This must be because energy is transferred as heat, I should be able to calculate the temperature change and then measure it...

| 1 | 2 | 3 | 4 | 5 | 6 | 7 | 8 | exceptional performance |

Likely level at Sc1

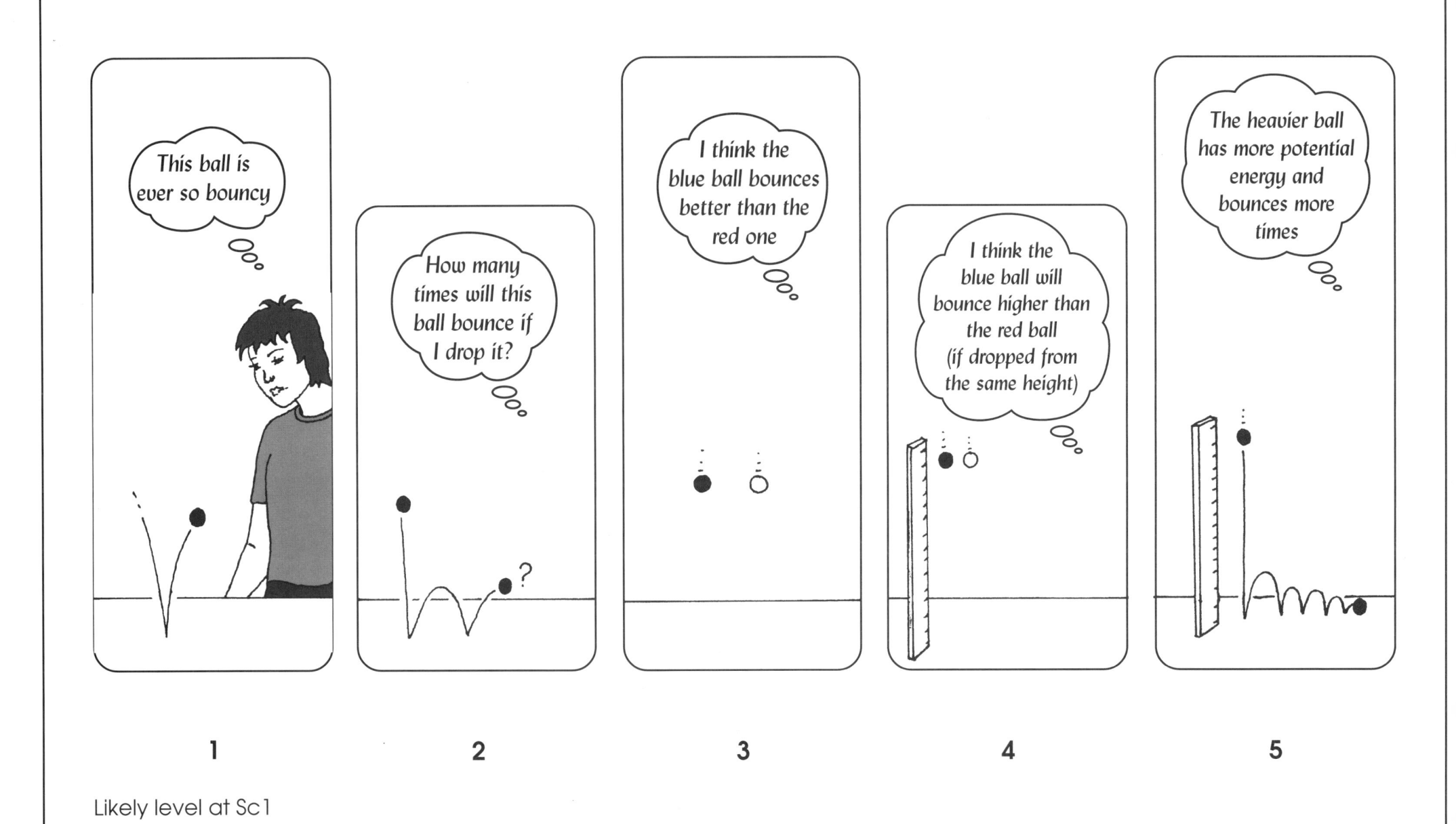

This ball is ever so bouncy	*How many times will this ball bounce if I drop it?*	*I think the blue ball bounces better than the red one*	*I think the blue ball will bounce higher than the red ball (if dropped from the same height)*	*The heavier ball has more potential energy and bounces more times*
1	2	3	4	5

Likely level at Sc1

Indicators of Levelness - Bouncing Ball Activity

	planning	obtaining evidence	analysing evidence and drawing conclusions	evaluating evidence
2	how many times will the ball bounce if I drop it?	I will mark height of bounce on a wall	each bounce is smaller than the one before	I expected it to bounce for much longer
3	I think the blue ball will bounce better than the red one because it's not so squashy	I will use a metre rule to measure the bounce	the blue ball bounces higher than the red ball - squashiness doesn't make a good bouncer	the test told me that the blue ball bounced higher
4	because they are different sizes one ball will bounce higher than the other	I will mark the starting position and the bounce height on the metre rule	the bars on the bar chart show that bigger balls bounce higher	the test was fair because I dropped them from the same heights
5	the heavier ball has more potential energy and will bounce more than a light ball	I will use different starting positions on the metre rule	the balls dropped at 10cm steps from 10cm to 100cm show that height of starting position is important because that affects it's energy.	two of the results can't fit the pattern in my results table perhaps I've got the measurements wrong

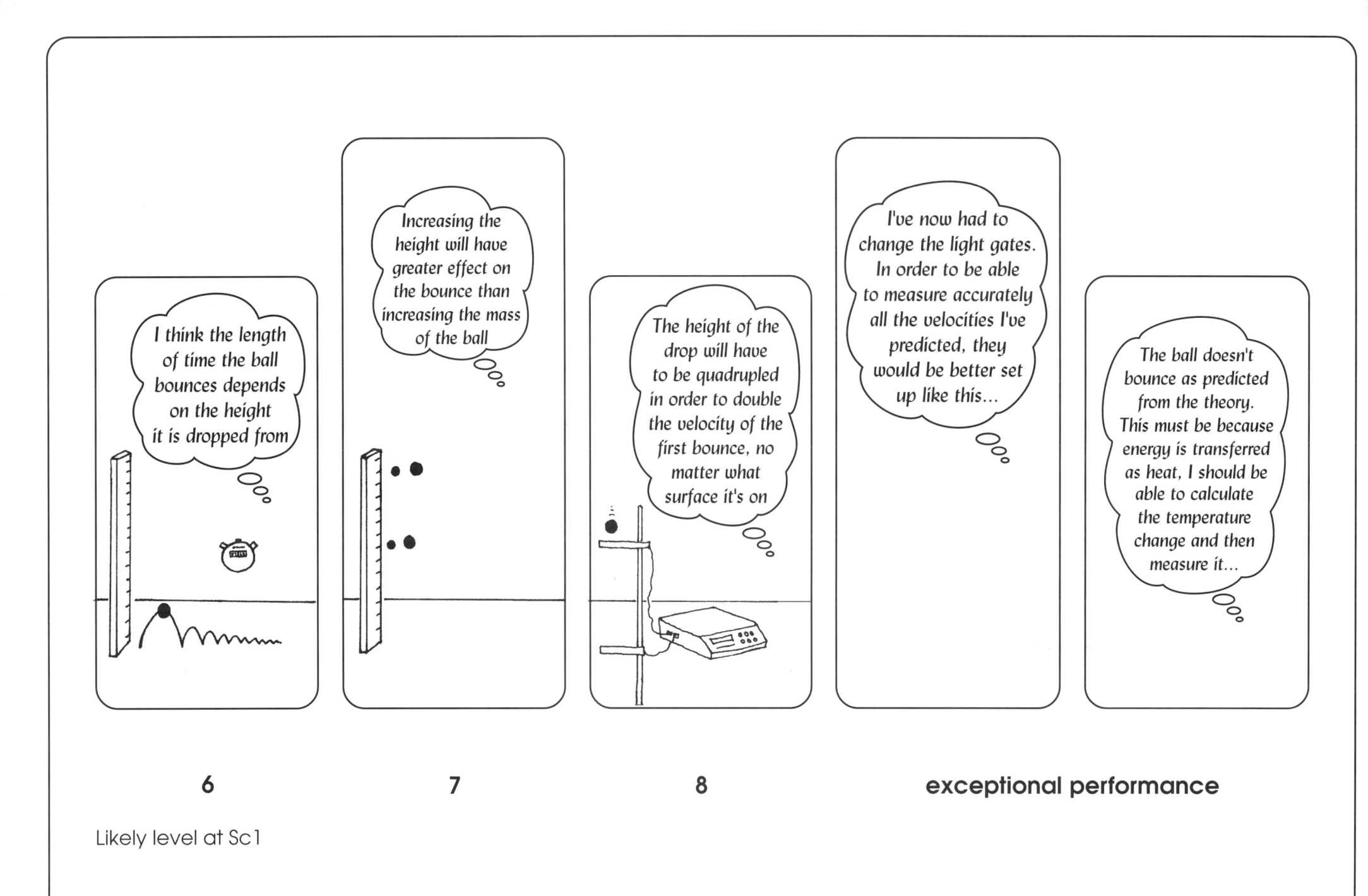

I think the length of time the ball bounces depends on the height it is dropped from	*Increasing the height will have greater effect on the bounce than increasing the mass of the ball*	*The height of the drop will have to be quadrupled in order to double the velocity of the first bounce, no matter what surface it's on*	*I've now had to change the light gates. In order to be able to measure accurately all the velocities I've predicted, they would be better set up like this...*	*The ball doesn't bounce as predicted from the theory. This must be because energy is transferred as heat, I should be able to calculate the temperature change and then measure it...*
6	**7**	**8**		**exceptional performance**

Likely level at Sc1

Indicators of Levelness - Bouncing Ball Activity

	planning	obtaining evidence	analysing evidence and drawing conclusions	evaluating evidence
6	the length of time the ball bounces depends on the height it is dropped from, the higher the drop the longer it will bounce	I will use a metre rule with millimetres and a digital watch with 1000ths of a second	dropping the ball from a greater height gives it more energy this makes it bounce longer	two of the results don't lie close enough to the line in my graph perhaps I've got the measurements wrong
7	as well as bounce time I will investigate the surface the ball bounces on	I will adopt a different scale I will get better results if I drop it in 5cm steps	we're not sure how much we can trust the results for different masses because we can't prove balls made of the same rubber, although line of best fit in the graph shows that height has the greatest effect	it was necessary to repeat each measurement 5 times in order to take an average...
8	I will set up light gates so they can record the range of velocities I expect	I could also try measuring the height of the bounce to see if the pattern in the velocities is confirmed	uses light gates to measure velocity to $\pm 1 cms^{-1}$ and ensures data/graphs/tables approximate to this error	the important measurement is the movement during the second half of the journey to ensure consistent terminal velocity is reached, I will repeat measurements across this range
E	I will compare the tennis ball performance with this data sheet from Addibounce Ltd	I asked the technician how to set up light gates for maximum sensitivity I will test reliability as I take measurements by repeating for consistent results	plots $(height)^2$ vs velocity graph to explore the expected relationship	my calculations show that the energy transferred as heat could result in a temperature change I need to investigate this further

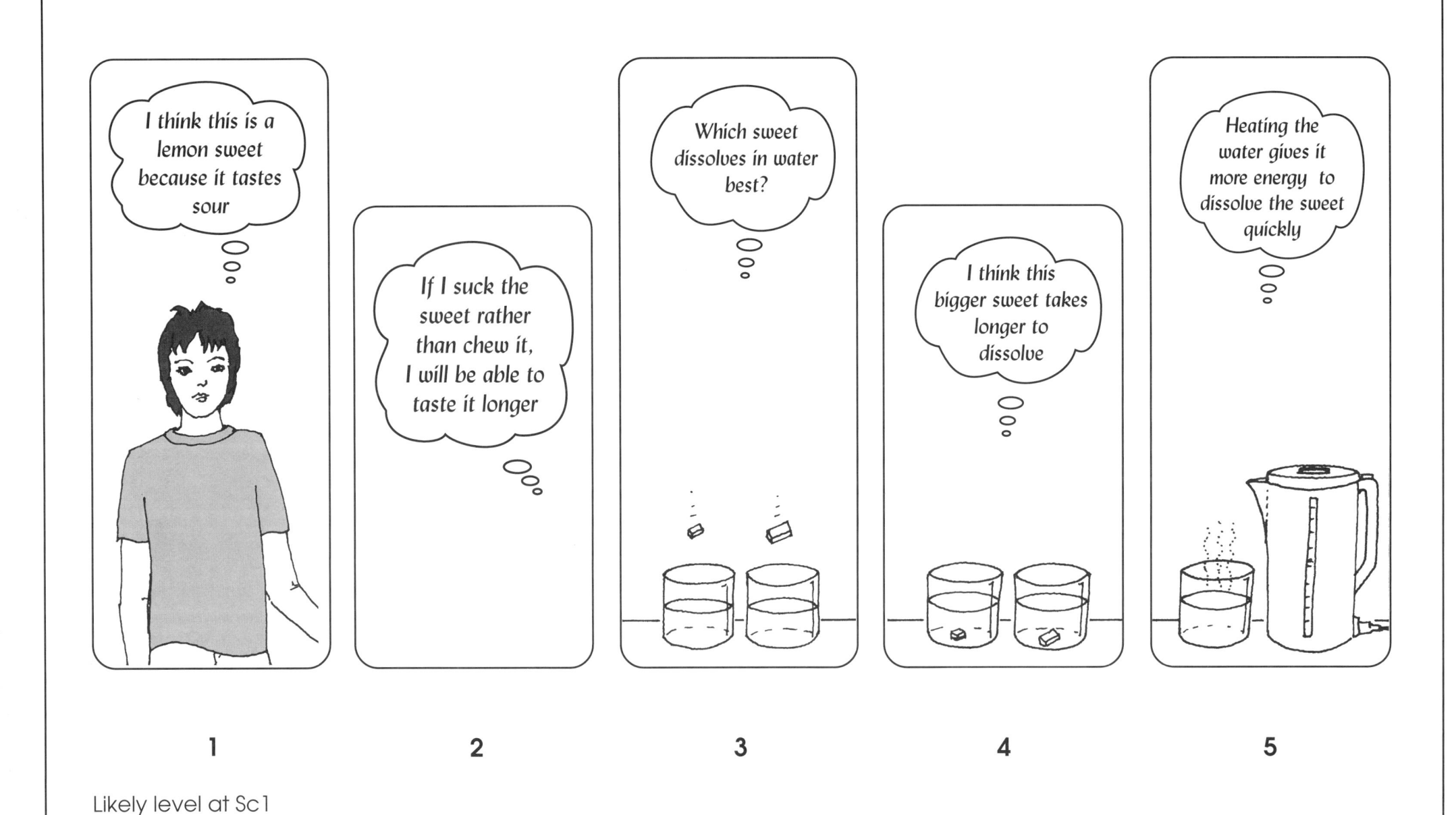

1	2	3	4	5
I think this is a lemon sweet because it tastes sour	*If I suck the sweet rather than chew it, I will be able to taste it longer*	*Which sweet dissolves in water best?*	*I think this bigger sweet takes longer to dissolve*	*Heating the water gives it more energy to dissolve the sweet quickly*

Likely level at Sc1

Indicators of Levelness - Solubility Activity

	planning	obtaining evidence	analysing evidence and drawing conclusions	evaluating evidence
2	predicts - if I suck the sweet rather than chew it, it will last longer	I will tell my friend which lasted longest	the sweet has both a sharp and a sweet flavour	I expected that chewing would make the sweet disappear quickly
3	asks which sweet will dissolve best in water	uses a clock to measure how many minutes it takes to dissolve	the smallest sweets dissolve the quickest	I should have used the same amount of water each time
4	suggests this bigger sweet will take longer to dissolve	I will tell my friend when to start and stop the clock to measure seconds	can use data collected to relate size of sweet to length of time to dissolve	ensures that equal amounts of water were used and that the water was stirred whilst making measurements
5	says that heating the water gives it more energy to dissolve the sweet, so it will dissolve quicker	I will use a timer and a thermometer to measure the time to dissolve in 20°C, 40°C, 60°C, 80°C and 100°C	uses a line graph at each temperature to identify patterns in the results	repeats measurements at each temperature to test reliability of results

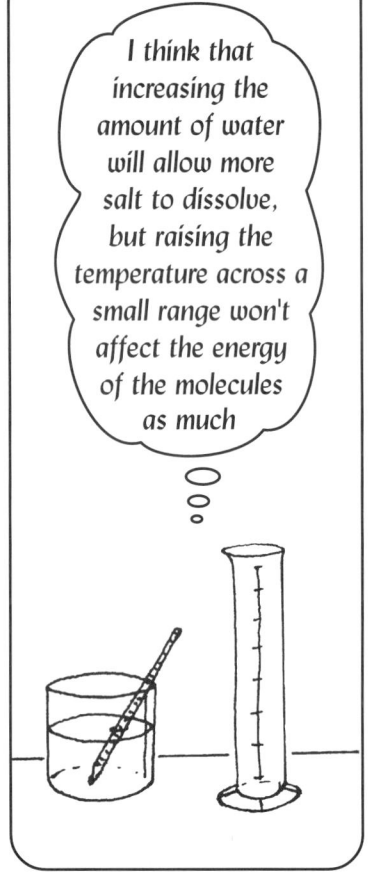

The hotter the water the shorter the time it will take to dissolve the sweet

I think that increasing the amount of water will allow more salt to dissolve, but raising the temperature across a small range won't affect the energy of the molecules as much

I have predicted the solubility at several temperatures and planned my investigation

In order to test my predictions accurately I had to improve the accuracy of the measurements and to repeat them in order to take an average

I'm going to check the solubility of other sodium salts and other chlorides to find out whether it's the sodium ion or chloride ion or both that determine the solubility curve

6 **7** **8** **exceptional performance**

Likely level at Sc1

100

Indicators of Levelness - Solubility Activity

	planning	obtaining evidence	analysing evidence and drawing conclusions	evaluating evidence
6	says that the higher the temperature the faster sweets will dissolve	I will measure mass in graphs and temperature in °C and use a mechanical stirrer	identifies patterns in graphs produced and explains them using particulate knowledge and understanding	uses graphs to identify measurements that do not fit the pattern
7	predicts that increasing the volume of water will dissolve more salt, but that changing the temperature of the water from 20°C to 40°C won't increase it so much	accurately measures the solubility of sodium chloride in 50g and 100g of water at 20°C and 40°C	identifies a possible pattern in results but recognises more intermediate measurements are needed to confirm shape of graph	decides whether to take additional measurements at 10°C, 30°C, 50°C, 70°C and 100°C to confirm pattern in results
8	from previous results can interpolate to predict the solubility of sodium chloride at 30°C and 35°C, and can explain how to carry out the investigations accurately at these temperatures	I will measure mass of dissolving solute accurately in 100cm^3 of water at specific temperatures	recognises that patterns across 5°C intervals can contrubute to overall conclusion but not at 2°C intervals	can explain detailed aspects of the investigation, such as the need to measure the mass of soluent the mass of solvent used rather than volume of solvent or solution
E	can predict solubility of sodium chloride at other temperatures and suggests taking sufficient measurements to plot an accurate solubility curve	carries out data search on solubility of sodium salts and chlorides; measures the solubility of potassium chloride and sodium fluoride	systematically uses graphs to determine the solubility and disusses how to account for the effect of evaporation of solvent at higher temperatures	compare the solubility curves of NaCl, NaF & KCl with other data to find any correlations; correlation temporarily suggests that the solubility of NaCl is a function of interactions between both Na$^+$ & Cl$^-$ ions & water molecules

Some Possible Milestones - Assessing Sc1

	planning	obtaining evidence
2	responds to suggestions of how to find things out	uses simple equipment provided (eg magnifier)
3	may make simple predictions where appropriate decides what observations and measurements to make	measures quantities such as length and mass
4	predictions when made are not necessarily based on scientific knowledge and understanding **knows how to change one factor whilst keeping some others constant**	**select equipment** makes a series of observations and measurements adequate for the task
5	**when appropriate makes predictions based on scientific knowledge and understanding** confidently varies one factor whilst others are controlled	measures correctly to 1°C, 1 newton or uses digital meters appropriately
6	routinely identifies key factors, based securely on knowledge and understanding	makes observations and measures accurately using instruments with adequate precision for the needs of the task
7	**identifies key factors even in complex situations involving a range of factors some of which it may not be possible to control**	uses a wide range of apparatus and instruments with precision
8	**recognises the need for different strategies** when it is difficult to control factors or when factors can be precisely controlled	collects quantitive data which is precise enough to allow mathematical applications such as proportionality when appropriate
E	makes use of information from a range of relevant sources	decides on the degree of precision required by investigations and work to that degree of precision

	analysing evidence and drawing conclusions	evaluating evidence
2	compares things uses simple tables	compares what happened with what they expected "I was right"
3	**states what they have found out from their work (= simple conclusion)** simple patterns in observations are identified eg all these leaves have jagged edges	recognises fairness/unfairness
4	routine use of barcharts and simple graphs to present data **notices patterns when drawing conclusions**	begins to describe why they obtained results (using because statements)
5	line graphs have more points and complex scales (than level 4) relates conclusions to simple scientific knowledge	recognises that measurements may need to be repeated offers explanations for any differences in results
6	**explains conclusions using scientific knowledge and understanding**	**identifies observations and measurements that do not fit main pattern or trend** considers range and number of observations needed
7	**uses line of best fit on graph** recognises evidence is sufficient for firm conclusions to be drawn or that other factors affect results	recognises the need for reliable data and attempts to obtain it
8	**critical analysis of data/graphs/tables** systematic consideration of all the data	**decides which observations and measurements are relevant includes suitable detail, but irrelevant material is omitted**
E	concentrates on the most salient points in interpretation and explanation	**explains how additional data could be collected to test the conclusion**

Summative Assessment

The strategies for assessment outlined so far in the book make up the constituent aspects of formative assessment. This type of assessment is continuously taking place in the classroom whether the teacher makes a note of achievement or not, and can be planned by the teacher to ensure effective teaching and learning occurs. However, teachers will want to make snap-shot judgements of childrens' achievements so that they can be recorded at some periodic date or for the purposes of reporting to parents. This summative judgement can be made using three possible approaches before using the level descriptions of the National Curriculum in England and Wales:

- use lines of progress, possibly monitored by pupils themselves (chapters 4 and 10) to indicate the most likely end of key stage level

- use indicators of levelness (chapter 9) to suggest a likely end of key stage level

- use milestones in Sc1 (end of chapter 9) to indicate the most likely end of key stage level

Teachers can then use the level descriptions for Sc1 in the Science Orders. They will firstly look at the likely level description and confirm their professional judgement by looking at the level above and the level below. They will finally decide which is the best fit description given the various strengths and weaknesses shown across a range of contexts over a period of time.

At KS1, KS2 and KS3 summative decisions are **NOT** made by mathematical aggregations, but by consulting level descriptions.

I use lines of progress for detailed long term planning

I use indicators of levelness for medium term planning

I use milestones in Sc1 for short term planning

These give the first points of reference to the level description. Then I look for the best-fit description.

Summative assessment arrangements at the end of KS4 are defined by the course work assessment arrangements for GCSE. (see page 38)

Chapter 10

How Can We Help Children To Assess Their Own Progress?

page	106	How Can Children be Helped to Develop their Experimental and Investigative abilities?
	107	Things to Think About when Reporting your Experiment or Investigation
	109	Learner Self Assessment
	110	In my practical science work I can...

How Can Children be Helped to Develop their Experimental and Investigative Abilities?

In all kinds of learning it is important that children understand what they are expected to achieve and to recognise when they have achieved it. So too in scientific investigation. This is even more so as children mature, become more independent and can take even greater responsibility for their learning.

If children are to progress efficiently in scientific investigation they need to be specifically taught the skills of investigation (the use of investigation planning sheets is just one example of this). They also need to know the targets they are working towards. Within the framework of the Science Orders of the National Curriculum this means children understanding something of the level descriptions for Experimental and Investigative Science and the points of progression within them.

Having a copy of those level descriptions just as they stand is inappropriate for children; it takes teachers working with those statements a considerable time before they feel confident in their understanding. Few children would understand much of them without a lot of assistance.

It can be helpful if children have access to appropriate lines of progress, reworded in terms that they can easily understand. This will help them to know where they are going in their learning and when they have achieved their goal, possible examples are printed on pages 110 to 112.

Simply worded statements of progression help the learning objectives to be understood

Things to Think About when Reporting your Experiment or Investigation

Helping you Improve from Level 3 to Level 6

- ✓ What was your idea ?
- ✓ Were you able to predict any measurements or pattern before you started?
- ✓ What scientific knowledge or theory is your investigation based on?

- ✓ What did you need to keep constant to make it a fair test?
- ✓ What factor did you deliberately change (the input or independent variable)?
- ✓ What other factors did you observe or measure (the output or independent variables)?
- ✓ What range of measurements did you take?
- ✓ How did you make sure the measurements were accurate enough?
- ✓ Have you recorded all the important observations and measurements?

- ✓ What pattern did you find in your results (including graphs)? Did any results not match the pattern?
- ✓ Does your graph show the main pattern as clearly as possible?
- ✓ What do your results mean?
- ✓ How accurate and reliable are your results?

This page is copyright waived

Things to Think About when Reporting your Experiment or Investigation

Helping you to Reach Levels 5 - 10

- ✓ What idea or hypothesis were you investigating?
- ✓ Had you predicted any measurements or patterns at the start?
- ✓ What scientific knowledge or theory was your investigation based on?
- ✓ Did you change your hypothesis during the investigation or go on to investigate another one?
- ✓ How did you organise the investigation to make sure you got accurate and reliable results?

- ✓ What (variables) did you need to keep constant?
- ✓ What were the input (independent) and outcome (dependent) variables that you measured?
- ✓ What were the range of measurements that you took? Why?
- ✓ How did you make sure that your measurements were accurate enough?
- ✓ What pre-testing did you need to do in order to decide on the exact details of the investigation?
- ✓ Have you recorded all the important observations and measurements, concentrating on the most important features?

- ✓ What patterns did you find in your results (including maths and graph patterns)?
- ✓ What results didn't match this pattern? How did you deal with these odd results?
- ✓ What do your results mean?
- ✓ How accurate and reliable are your results and conclusions?
- ✓ What do your results tell you about the idea/hypothesis/prediction/theory that you were investigating?

This page is copyright waived

Learner Self Assessment

Many children are capable of playing a significant role in assessing their own learning and gain by the experience. Involvement in self assessment requires the learner to realise more fully the goals of their learning and to reflect on progress they have made in order to motivate them towards further achievement.

Older children in particular who are becoming more independent in their learning, could benefit from the advice in this chapter. The following three pages are intended to help children assess how far they have progressed in experimental and investigative work, each page being targetted at a particular range of achievement. Care must be taken to prevent children gaining the false impression from the regular shape of the matrix that learning progresses in even-sized steps or that progress occurs in all aspects in synchrony.

You may find the pages helpful in a number of ways:

- pupils could keep a copy in their exercise books or folders and mark off their achievements as they progress through the year

- pupils could keep it as part of a record of achievement

- the pupil's record could be used as the basis of dialogue between teacher and pupil about progress

- extracts could be cut-and-paste to custom make progress sheets for specific aspects of Sc1

- photo enlargement could be used to produce a poster for class use

- teachers less experienced in teaching Sc1 may find the less formal language helpful in their formative assessment

- sentences could be extracted as a source of simply worded learning objectives for practical activities

In my practical science work I can...

	2	3	4	5
considering factors and fair testing	follow other people's ideas or talk about how to find things out	make my own suggestions for tests sometimes do a fair test	do my own fair test change one factor and keep the other factors the same	always identify the key factors in my fair tests
resourcing	sometimes say some of the equipment I need, if I'm given a hint	suggest most of the equipment I will need	plan what equipment I will need before I start	always plan the equipment I need, even for more complicated tests
predicting	think about what might happen in an experiment	sometimes say what might happen before they do happen	say what might happen and explain why I think they will happen	use what I have learnt to predict what will happen
using equipment	use some equipment such as jars and spoons that I'm given	use ruler, thermometer, scales if I'm given them	choose the equipment I need	always choose the right piece of equipment and use it the correct way
observing and measuring	remember a list of things I have noticed	notice things carefully and use simple equipment	notice the important things and measure the right things to finish my test	make accurate observations and measurements and repeat them if necessary
organising evidence	make a chart or table	describe what happened set out my results clearly in lists, tables etc	set out clear accurate results in tables, bar charts and simple line graphs	set out my results logically in the best way draw accurate line graphs
analysing and explaining	compare some of the things I have noticed	say what has happened and any simple patterns I've noticed say what I've found out	find patterns in my results use what I've learnt to help explain what happened	state my conclusion and explain why it matches my results think about what I've learnt to help my explanation
evaluating	compare what did happen with what I thought would happen	say when a test is unfair	describe why I obtained my results	say when I need to repeat my results or use an average offer explanations for any differences in results
context and scale	carry out simple tests that I've been told about	carry out simple fair tests or other tests	carry out fair test where I change one factor and keep some others the same	carry out investigations where I know the main variables/factors

In my practical science work I can...

	4	5	6	7
considering factors and fair testing	do my own fair test change one factor and keep the other factors the same	always identify the key factors in my fair tests	use my knowledge of science to identify the key factors	use my knowledge of science to identify the key factors from amongst many
resourcing	plan what equipment I will need before I start	always plan the equipment I need, even for more complicated tests	plan what equipment I'll need and how I'm going to use it to get the best results	use equipment with appropriate procedures to get reliable results
predicting	say what might happen and explain why I think they will happen	use what I have learnt to predict what will happen	use my knowledge of science to predict effect of input variable on outcome variable or to work out further results if I did them	use my knowledge of science to predict even in situations where factors are difficult to control
using equipment	choose the equipment I need	always choose the right piece of equipment and use it the correct way	always select the correct equipment and use it properly to get accurate results	use more complicated apparatus with accuracy
observing and measuring	notice the important things and measure the right things to finish my test	make accurate observations and measurements and repeat them if necessary	measure accurately, often in decimals if necessary make enough observations or measurement to get sensible results	collect accurate results in a logical way spot places where it looks like more results are needed
organising evidence	set out clear accurate results in tables, bar charts and simple line graphs	set out my results logically in the best way draw accurate line graphs	select the best scales for line graphs to give the clearest results	use lines of best fit on graphs where needed
analysing and explaining	find patterns in my results use what I've learnt to help explain what happened	state my conclusion and explain why it matches my results think about what I've learnt to help my explanation	explain my conclusion and why it matches my results, using my knowledge of science	explain my conclusion using my knowledge of science think about whether I have enough evidence for conclusion
evaluating	describe why I obtained my results	say when I need to repeat my results or use an average offer explanations for any differences in results	say why I collected the results I did spot results that don't match the pattern in the rest	always check reliability of my results for maximum accuracy check if I have enough results
context and scale	carry out fair test where I change one factor and keep some others the same	carry out investigations where I know the main variables/factors	carry out an investigation where key factors are based on knowledge and understanding	carry out lots of different investigations involving a range of factors

This page is copyright waived

In my practical science work I can...

	6	7	8	exceptional
considering factors and fair testing	use my knowledge of science to identify the key factors	use my knowledge of science to identify the key factors from amongst many	know when to use a different approach and to use my knowledge of science to work out my strategy	use additional information from other sources to help plan my strategy
resourcing	plan what equipment I'll need and how I'm going to use it to get the best results	use equipment with appropriate procedures to get reliable results	use equipment which will enable accurate calculations of functions such as proportionality	plan and use equipment which has a degree of precision to enable the collection of accurate and reliable results
predicting	use my knowledge of science to predict effect of input variable on outcome variable or to work out further results if I did them	use my knowledge of science to predict even in situations where factors are difficult to control	use knowledge of science to predict for factors precisely controlled and difficult to control	use information from a range of relevant sources to support my prediction
using equipment	always select the correct equipment and use it properly to get accurate results	use more complicated apparatus with accuracy	always use more complicated apparatus with skill and precision	use any piece of complicated or sensitive apparatus with skill and accuracy to a high degree of precision
observing and measuring	measure accurately, often in decimals if necessary make enough observations or measurement to get sensible results	collect accurate results in a logical way spot places where it looks like more results are needed	sort out the relevant from irrelevant details collect measurements accurate enough for the calculations required	sort out the relevant from irrelevant details collect measurements accurate enough for the calculations required
organising evidence	select the best scales for line graphs to give the clearest results	use lines of best fit on graphs where needed	make allowance for anomalous results when drawing graphs	record things precisely and concisely explain anomalous results using science knowledge and understanding
analysing and explaining	explain my conclusion and why it matches my results, using my knowledge of science	explain my conclusion using my knowledge of science think about whether I have enough evidence for conclusion	use my knowledge of science to draw conclusions, even given any shortcomings of the evidence	think critically about my data and its most important features think whether my conclusion is safe or needs further testing
evaluating	say why I collected the results I did spot results that don't match the pattern in the rest	always check reliability of my results for maximum accuracy check if I have enough results	identify the most important and relevant data from the rest identify and try to explain anomolous results	explain clearly how and why I dealt with anomalous results explain further evidence I need to be more certain about conclusion
context and scale	carry out an investigation where key factors are based on knowledge and understanding	carry out lots of different investigations involving a range of factors	carry out complicated investigations which involve different strategies	carry out complicated investigations which involve different strategies, even if the work is new to me